POLAR BEARS
AND PENGUINS

*Transforming even the most polarised
organisation into a High Performing Culture
where a diverse group of employees can
thrive in any weather condition*

KEVIN CRAIG & **SUSAN STEVENSON**
WITH **CARL GOULD**

Craig, Kevin; Stevenson, Susan
Polar Bears and Penguins: Transforming even the most polarised organisation into a High Performing Culture where a diverse group of employees can thrive in any weather condition

First Edition
ISBN: 978-1-9998226-0-6

Library of Congress Control Number: 2017914031

Legal Deposit and the Library of Trinity College Dublin
The British Library

Cover and interior design by Kendra Cagle

Published by Grip Publishing.

For More information, please visit:
www.pbpbooks.com

DEDICATION

....

To my lovely patient wife, Khulood who can now finally see this book in real life; I've talked about it ever since we first met in 2013. To my dear late Mother who passed away in June 2016, a huge inspiration to me and my source of linguist excellence, to my Father for his continuous encouragement, my late grandfather for his courage and determination and more recently my very special daughter, baby Mai, who sadly passed away a week after she was born and taught me the meaning of true love.

Kevin S. Craig

....

To my dear late Mother who always said "I don't know what to tell my friends when they ask me what you do in your consulting. What I do know, is that you help people and companies". This is for you Mom!

Susan J. Stevenson

"Polar Bears and Penguins is a wonderful book providing leaders with the principles, tools and techniques to change their business and the people within it to be a unified, aligned and productive community. This is a practical and helpful book filled with invaluable insights and information that no leader can afford to ignore."

Karen Kimsey-House | Co-Founder CTI
and Co-Author of *Co-Active Coaching*

"I have had the privilege of experiencing this work first hand when navigating my organisation through uncharted waters. I recommend this book to any CEO who has a diverse organisation and desires a high performing culture."

Mohamed Bin Isa Al Khalifa | Former CEO Batelco Group

"This is an excellent book which provides practical tools and techniques to understand the critical importance of culture and how it impacts business results through the "engagement of your people". It will give you the framework required to guide your leaders and employees on a journey that will align commonalities and differences, resulting in a high performing team."

Carolyn Clark | Senior Vice President, Talent & Culture,
North & Central America, Accor Hotels

"This is a great book for entrepreneurs and business leaders wether you are just starting out or a seasoned professional who is aiming to get the best results out of your business. I highly recommend this book."

Sofyan Almoayed | Managing Director,
Khalid Almoayed & Sons

TABLE OF CONTENTS

....

INTRODUCTION

. . . .

During a 1992 visit to Australia, American President George H.W. Bush greeted a group of locals through the window of his armoured car by raising two fingers to form a "V." In America this is understood to mean "Victory" or even "Peace." But in Australia it is an extremely obscene gesture, the equivalent in the United States to extending the middle finger. Completely unintentionally, a major head of state insulted an entire nation.

Not too long ago, most of us would only run the risk of such an embarrassing mistake if we went abroad on vacation. The rest of the time, we interacted—particularly in our professional lives—almost exclusively within a cultural framework with which we were deeply familiar. We didn't question the morals and norms that governed our behaviour at work any more than a fish would question the composition of the water in which it swam.

The global economy has changed all that. As more and more companies do business across international boundaries, executives and other business leaders find themselves overseeing groups of people from all over the world. While we might avoid the unintentional obscene gesture, we may be completely oblivious to a litany of inadvertent offenses and misunderstandings that could be occurring on a daily basis.

If corporate leaders do not deliberately build a culture in which a diverse ensemble of employees can thrive, the organisation will quickly become polarised. Polarised organisations can feel almost impossible to lead effectively. At best, they are characterised by high employee turnover, disengaged employees, and a general environment of distrust. At worst, you may find yourself dealing with employees who bully and sabotage one another, hurting performance and undermining the organisation's goals.

Polar Bears and Penguins in the Office

Most of the time, polarisation is the result of inexperience and unfamiliarity more than overt hostility among employees. Just like polar bears and penguins actually inhabit very similar climates but are naturally unaware of one another's existence, different groups of employees may share very similar needs but have absolutely no experience interacting with one another. They can only overcome that lack of understanding with the right leadership.

Beyond the inevitable challenges from within, multinational organisations also face complex environmental challenges that more homogenous organisations are often spared. Just as a storm or shift in climate may threaten the survival of a species, a political or economic crisis in a far corner of the world may threaten an organisation's future. Corporate leaders must be equipped to lead not just on sunny days, but through the sandstorms and blizzards as well.

The good news is that with the right awareness, skills and intentions, you can successfully prepare for the climate and weather changes that are beyond your control. Likewise, you can create an authentic and encouraging culture that allows polar bears and penguins to not only get along, but also work together productively. You can cultivate authentic relationships within your organisation that encourage people to come together in a crisis—instead of turning against one another—and improve performance in any season or storm.

To help you do this, we've created the "5 Step Roadmap to Acculturate"—transforming even the most polarised organisation into a high performing culture where a diverse group of employees can thrive in any weather conditions:

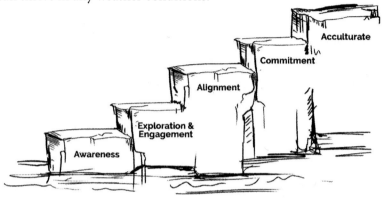

Image: 5 Step Roadmap to Acculturate

Throughout this book, we use an ICE™ metaphor representing the platform in which your organisation sits.

Lots of factors affect the condition of the organisational platform (**I**nfrastructure, **C**onsciousness and **E**co-Wisdom™), some within our control—like the organisational culture—and some out of our control like shifts in the market or economic climate.

We've all seen the picture of the iceberg that shows only a small portion above the surface of the water. And the same is true of the environment of organisations: we see the surface-level interactions between people and we see the overall performance of each department. But what's going on underneath? Is the ICE™ solid and stable, providing a secure foundation for growth? Or is the ICE™ thinning to the point where a sudden crisis will break everything to pieces? This book will teach you how to look beneath the surface to assess your ICE™, how to spot fissures or weak spots and what to do about them. You'll learn to strengthen the ICE™ so everyone can thrive together.

Transforming Organisational Consciousness

This book is ultimately about transformation. Many organisations become stuck in unhealthy patterns of doing business the way individuals become stuck in unhealthy lifestyles. Just as weight loss and dietary changes take time, genuine organisational transformation requires effort and investment. This book is not a magic diet pill that pledges to melt the pounds away overnight; it's about teaching you to transform the environment of your organisation into a high performing culture where a diverse group of employees can thrive in any weather conditions.

As authors of this book, we have decades of experience bridging cultural gaps that reach from North America to the UK and the Middle and Far East. We have dealt with challenges as dramatic as a head of state insulting a crowd and as minor as a misunderstanding in the break room. Our experience spans retail, automotive, manufacturing, hospitality, banking and finance, communications and IT, oil and gas, aviation and logistics. We have helped executive and managerial leaders navigate the storms and seasonal changes associated with many industries, and we've also helped them to align diverse workforces to pursue a common purpose and goal, thus achieving their full potential.

Although we pay particular attention to cultural differences in the work place, many factors can contribute to organisational polarity. A change in leadership, the acquisition of one company by another and many other industry changes can all cause employees to become divided into factions working against each other instead of together. Our techniques and skills can be applied to any of these scenarios to bring greater unity, more effective cooperation and better results.

This book will give you principles, techniques and skills to assess the culture of your organisation and turn even the most polarised workplace into that of an aligned, productive community, but it will require commitment and engagement on your part. You will learn the skills and information you need to build relationships and systems to ensure that you steer your people, your processes and products in the right direction. And finally, this book will introduce you to further resources to make sure that your company not only reaches its goals, but exceeds them.

STEP 1

. . . .

AWARENESS

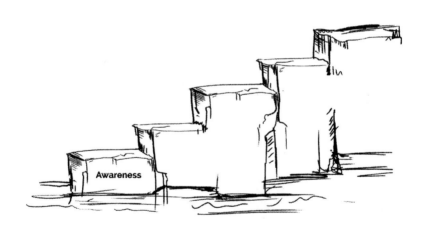

CHAPTER 1

....

Guiding Principles for a High Performing Culture

To transform an organisation, you must first be aware of its current state and how it got that way. How do we become aware? Everyone has five senses, but we don't all use them in the same manner. A father may notice that his child seems upset after school, but what does he do with that observation? He can ignore the child's mood completely, assuming it will go away on its own. He can make a mental note of the child's behaviour and monitor it from a distance throughout the afternoon.

The father can also ask the child a question, such as, "How was school today?" (Anecdotal evidence strongly suggests that the child will answer, "Fine.") Or he can ask an even more powerful question, such as, "What was the most challenging part of school today?" The answer to this question may go a long way toward shedding some light on the source of the child's apparent distress without coming across as an interrogation.

However the father chooses to deal with (or not deal with) the child, there are certain guiding principles at work. In families, these principles are rarely articulated; they are simply assumed. The father is not going to stop being the child's parent, regardless of the cause of the child's distress. A thoughtful father will pay attention to the child when he comes home from school, rather than taking a phone call or reading the paper. The father who asks about the most challenging part of the school day shows his willingness to have a deeper conversation with his son, probing beneath the surface. Unless the boy's troubles are coming from a highly unusual source, the father will feel fully confident that they can be handled with the emotional support and resources the family already possesses.

Leaders who are able to transform organisations successfully begin with a similar set of guiding principles. They are completely **committed** to their organisation and to their employees. They are **fully present** with what is happening at the moment instead of being constantly distracted or focused on peripheral issues. Transformational leaders engage in **deep dialogue** with their colleagues and employees to ensure that each one has an opportunity to air their concerns and feel heard, and they **look for the answers to the challenges from within** the organisation, rather than from the outside.

The more diverse your organisation, the more vital these guiding principles will be in cultivating a high performing culture. Greater diversity means the people involved come to the table with fewer shared assumptions about everything from authority and gender relations to work/family balance and even workplace etiquette. While you can't always predict which challenges your company will encounter, you can prepare for them by proactively creating an environment where everyone pulls together instead of pushing apart. This chapter elaborates on the guiding principles leaders need, to do just that. All leaders have to make tough—even unpopular—decisions, so you want to be sure you are making the right call for the right reasons.

The Rudderless Ship

Sitting on a boat on a clear, still day can be very relaxing. If your boat is on a lake or in a protected bay, you may not even need to steer. You can simply drift along with the current and enjoy the view. But if the wind picks up or a storm appears over the horizon, you're going to need to be able to guide that boat exactly where you want it to go immediately.

Even good leaders can sometimes allow the boat to drift. It's easy to become complacent with the status quo if you are getting acceptable results for the moment. When there isn't a crisis, it is very tempting to assume that everything fine. What happens when that storm hits? Will the culture of your company be strong enough to prompt everyone to work together to keep the ship steady? Or will it suddenly become every man for himself?

Every organisation has a set of norms that shape its employees' performance and their ability to handle challenges. These norms are created regardless of the attention given to them by the leadership of the organisation. If leaders do not articulate and incentivise the culture they desire, they are passively creating the culture they probably do not want. But sometimes they may not realise this until a storm hits.

We all want to cultivate an environment that encourages everyone to contribute his best so that the organisation in turn can be the best it can be. But without being **committed, fully present with what is, engaging in deep dialogue,** and **looking for answers within,** we are leaving the culture of our organisation up to chance. Transformational leaders are able to proactively shape their organisation with intention and purpose, rather than waiting for a crisis and then merely reacting to it.

Different people view authority very differently, depending on their backgrounds. Some leaders try to assert their authority in a top-down fashion, forcing their employees to follow along or face punitive actions. Others may go to the opposite extreme, trying to befriend their employees rather than providing the leadership and vision they need. Often in diverse organisations, leaders must strike a delicate balance between these two extremes. These guiding principles will help you strike that balance, while ensuring the ship stays steady in all circumstances.

Be Committed

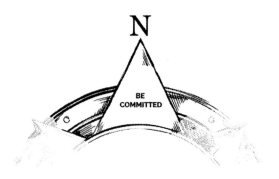

Interpersonal conflicts at the office can be difficult to deal with, especially when those conflicts cross cultures. Everyone puts on their best face during the interview process—both the leaders and the prospective employees—so coming to work can be a rude awakening for everyone concerned. Without commitment at all levels of an organisation, different individuals and even different departments will not work together to be their best. Unless you consciously cultivate strong relationships among your employees, the organisation will be a shipwreck waiting to happen.

To transform a group of people, you must be fully committed to them, the purpose of the organisation and to the goals you want to achieve. Part of becoming aware as a leader is assessing your own commitment and how that commitment is communicated to your employees. Are they confident that you care and that you are not going to be gone tomorrow? Can they trust your commitment to them and to what you are asking them to do?

In any relationship, commitment must precede trust. In some ways this is even truer of relationships at the office, because the work relationship is always one of choice. The organisation chooses to employ the employee, but the employees also get up every morning and choose to go and work for that organisation. It would seem that the employer is in the position of power here, because they hire, fire and sign the pay cheque. A quick look at the incredible costs of high employee turnover will demonstrate that organisations need committed, engaged, aligned employees as much as those employees need their pay cheques.

Commitment requires leaders to exercise their choices in the best interests of the organisation and those who work there, whatever that involves. The good news is, that commitment on the part of leadership encourages and nurtures commitment on the part of the employees. When they see and experience how truly committed you are to the transformation of the organisation so that all members can perform and contribute to their full potential, almost all will respond in kind.

How committed are you? Refer to questions 1-5 on the assessment at the end of this chapter.

Be Fully Present With What is

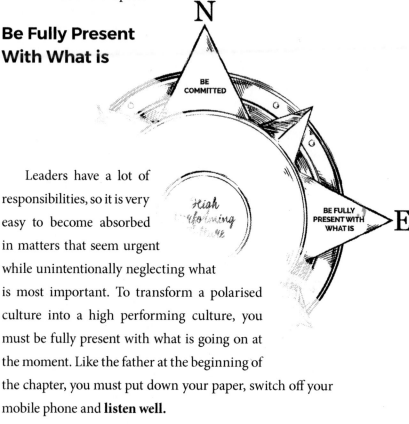

Leaders have a lot of responsibilities, so it is very easy to become absorbed in matters that seem urgent while unintentionally neglecting what is most important. To transform a polarised culture into a high performing culture, you must be fully present with what is going on at the moment. Like the father at the beginning of the chapter, you must put down your paper, switch off your mobile phone and **listen well.**

Many times, as consultants and facilitators, we don't know what we're dealing with until we're right in the middle of it. Someone could give you dozens of pages of data on a organisation or a department— including the demographic details of each employee and every number related to every aspect of performance. But this would still not tell you why a department or an organisation as a whole is polarised.

Often we are brought in to address a conflict or a misunderstanding in the middle levels of an organisation, only to discover that those employees are merely responding to the de-facto values at the top of the organisation. An organisation can say on paper that it values the opinions and contributions of all its employees. If in reality the leaders become agitated or angry in response to certain situations, the organisation will be governed by fear. And few things are as polarising as fear.

Until you are in the midst of the people themselves, paying attention and observing for days, weeks and even months, you will not have a full picture of what is really going on. This kind of presence requires **genuine curiosity.** You have to care enough about the organisation to want to get to the bottom of the mystery and determine what's really going on.

How present are you? Refer to the questions 6-10 on the assessment at the end of this chapter.

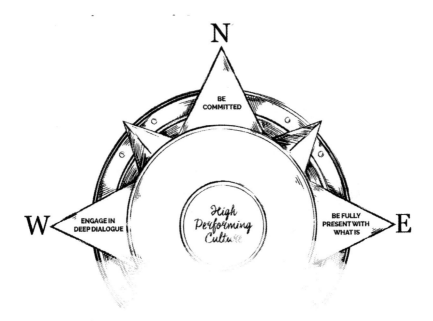

Deep dialogue requires focus and vulnerability. You cannot ask **powerful questions** without opening yourself up to honest answers. This requires that you, as a leader, be absolutely secure in who you are and in your own commitment to what is best for the organisation.

Deep dialogue also requires emotional intelligence—the ability to accurately read emotional cues from the person to whom you are speaking and to adjust your own behaviour accordingly. All of this is infinitely more challenging in a diverse environment. You can read books on how social customs vary from culture to culture, but the best training occurs in the school of experience and observation.

Many leaders may assume that deep dialogue must be direct and confrontational, but often just the opposite is true. In reality, many people become defensive or fearful when directly confronted about an issue, which does not build deeper connections or trust. The goal of deep dialogue is to ask **powerful questions** that will encourage your employees to speak freely and openly without feeling accused or interrogated.

Some industries and cultures are more accustomed to at least a few young leaders in the mix, but people elsewhere may find it difficult to accept young leadership. In a high performing culture, every voice—young and old—in the organisation has a chance to be heard. This is how the decision makers are able to maximise the collective knowledge of the people in the company and make it the best that it can be.

Now of course just because people get to be heard does not mean they will necessarily get their way, but it does mean that they are taken seriously and the organisation benefits from their information. High performing cultures are distinguished by having a mechanism whereby information can make its way rapidly to the top.

Allowing all voices to be truly heard requires that deep dialogue be part of the company's normal procedures. Remember to focus on what everyone—regardless of culture—has in common. Everyone wants to feel that they are contributing to the organisation and that their contribution is valued.

Ongoing deep dialogue is also important because, more often than not, corporate leadership tends to be reactionary. We are often brought in to deal with a particular issue that is really just a small part of what's actually going on in the organisation. This is not unlike going to the doctor to be treated for a rash, only to discover that there is an underlying infection causing the rash. You thought you needed a cream to apply to your skin, but you really needed some pills to eliminate the infection. Once the infection is dealt with, the rash will go away on its own.

Most of the time in diverse companies, these underlying issues go unaddressed. Sometimes they are too painful or they make us too uncomfortable to discuss. Leaders may not be able to imagine how to navigate through them, so they leave them covered up. Sometimes these issues are just too dull and boring, so the organisation initiates another reorganisation or a re-brand instead of addressing what's really going wrong.

Deep dialogue can be uncomfortable or even frightening for some people. But in high performing cultures, people are actually comfortable with being uncomfortable once in a while. This is realistic when leaders are demonstrating commitment and cultivating similar commitment within their employees.

How well do you engage in deep dialogue? Refer to questions 11-15 on the assessment at the end of this chapter.

Look for Answers Within

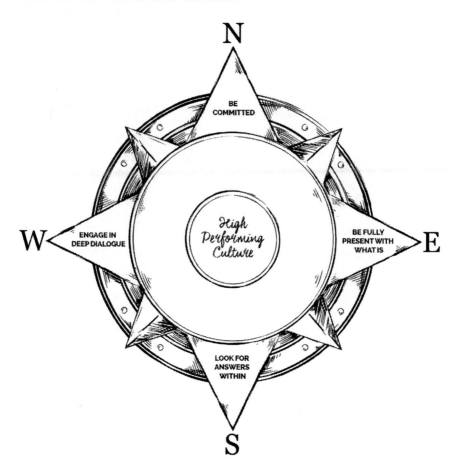

High performing cultures look for the answers to their challenges from within the organisation. This does not mean that they never employ outside help, but it does mean that the outside help is engaged to invest in the people that they already have.

High performing leaders are not constantly searching for the mythological "perfect employee" who will be able to perform well despite a dysfunctional organisational culture. Instead they are devoted to transforming their culture such that it gets the most

out of everyone they already have. None of this is to say
performing organisation will never have to fire anyone. Bu
fire, it is because that individual has failed the organisati
other way around.

Not every organisation wants to strive for high performance or to
be the very best it can be. But for those who are motivated to make the
organisation everything it can be—to build something that will retain
loyal employees, exceed customer expectations and weather any storm
that comes around—these guiding principles are irreplaceable. They
take time and effort to incorporate into one's leadership style, to be
sure, but they will deliver dividends that will be more than worth the
investment.

How well do you seek the answers from within your organisation?
Refer to questions 16-20 on the assessment on the next page.

Visit our online Leadership Guiding Principles Assessment at
www.pbpbooks.com/assessments

Guiding Principles Assessment

For each statement below, rank yourself on a scale of 1 to 5 where 1 is disagree and 5 is strongly agree:

Be Committed

#	QUESTION	Rank 1-5
1	I fully believe in the purpose/vision of my organisation.	
2	I have clearly articulated the purpose/vision of the organisation internally.	
3	I have clearly communicated the goals of the organisation internally.	
4	I fully live all of the company's core values.	
5	I am committed to regular formal (e.g. weekly meetings) & informal (e.g. floor walk about) communication throughout the entire organisation.	

Be Fully Present With What Is

#	QUESTION	Rank 1-5
6	I ask questions without expectations of the response.	
7	When I am communicating with others they have my full attention.	
8	When I interact with others I acknowledge their thoughts and feelings before responding.	
9	I genuinely care about understanding the person I am communicating with.	
10	If I am too distracted with other thoughts, I am honest with the other party that this is not the best time to have this conversation, and I reschedule when I can be fully present.	

Engage in Deep Dialogue

#	QUESTION	
11	I am able to appreciate the feelings and emotions in the room rather than allowing them to take me off-track.	
12	I am able to make appropriate decisions based on the emotional states of others.	
13	I demonstrate personal restraint when I experience powerful emotions (e.g. anger, frustration, joy) that could be distracting for others.	
14	I make sure I invite the quieter voices in the room to be heard before making decisions.	
15	I always ask questions that are open ended and provoke thought.	

Look for Answers Within

#	QUESTION	Rank 1-5
16	When I seek outside assistance it is my intention to make sure I develop the skills and knowledge of the people I already have in the organisation.	
17	I consult the people within my organisation for answers to our problems.	
18	I embrace difference of opinion(s) rather than allowing it to be a source of conflict.	
19	I am willing to let people know that I don't know all the answers.	
20	I always look for answers from within the organisation first before seeking outside assistance.	

Total number of each ranking: ☐ ☐ ☐ ☐ ☐

          x1   x2   x3   x4   x5

Multiply by the number above: ☐ ☐ ☐ ☐ ☐

Add all five numbers to determine the percentage score that reflects your readiness to embrace the journey: ☐ %

In terms of the effectiveness of a leadership team, our experience indicates that a team cohesiveness to these four guiding principles has far more impact on success than its level of experience or knowledge. In a few short words, being at least 75% strong in these principles is the biggest indicator of future success that your organisation can achieve in its transformation.

How do you Assess your team cohesiveness to these principles?

Collect the scores from each section as a team and identify the overall percentage strength for each principle knowing that you want to be at 75% or higher to be in the top quartile.Then ask the following questions for each principle:

What are you doing well as a team?

What do you need to be doing better as a team?

What do you need to stop doing?

What do you need to start doing?

CHAPTER 2

....

Beginning the Journey of Awareness

A lot of business books explain in great detail how to squeeze a greater number of euros, dollars or pounds out of your production processes to improve your bottom line. This is important: all organisations should strive to eliminate waste for the sake of their customers and stakeholders alike. Not all techniques that are typically prescribed to increase efficiency necessarily speak to the needs of a diverse workforce, nor will they help you when your organisation is overtaken by a transcendent event or crisis.

There was no Human Resources manual to help multi-national companies in the Middle East navigate the Arab Spring. For months on end, revolutionary fervour rooted in decades of political frustration overflowed into many corners of the Arab world. Emotions ran high, for both local and foreign workers, and their families were confused and scared. Some organisations ceased to operate during this time, effectively shutting their doors. Others were able to weather the storm and emerge on top.

The roadmap we outlined in the introduction will lead your organisation through the kind of transformation that enables a company not only to survive major, unpredictable challenges, but also to come out better than ever. This roadmap will allow a polarised organisation to become an aligned, connected community performing at its full potential.

Awareness, the first step of the roadmap, is only useful when it leads into the other steps. Consider geographical awareness for example. We can become aware of our physical surrounding in different ways. We can become experts on the characteristics of the place where we are, noting everything about the flora, fauna and terrain. Or we can learn about where we are in relationship to the rest of the world: our longitude and latitude and our distance from other cities and countries.

The first kind of awareness is concerned with the details of where you are right now. The second kind of awareness tells you where you are in relation to where you want to go. It is not awareness for its own sake, but rather awareness to determine how to get somewhere better. This is the kind of awareness that transformational leaders are after.

Toward the High Dream

In Japan, pedestrians stop at red lights even late at night, when there are no cars in sight. In Botswana, no one would dream of denying anyone—even a complete stranger—a glass of water if he or she asked. No one forces anyone to behave this way in these countries; it is simply part of the culture. The ultimate goal of organisational transformation is not to enforce high performing behaviours but to make them a central part of your organisation's culture.

At the end of the day, leaders must ask themselves what kind of company they want to build, and employees must ask themselves what kind of company they want to be part of. These questions go beyond the product or service the company provides to the environment where most of the employees will spend a huge portion of their waking hours. Google is a search engine, but it has created a corporate culture that has set it apart from other technology companies. It's not just a market leader; it's an inspiration to the entire industry.

The purpose of awareness is to move toward what we want the organisation to be. This is often referred to as the vision of the organisation. Unfortunately, most vision statements are formulated at a corporate retreat as part of a group writing exercise. These kinds of documents typically hold little meaning for those who create them, let alone for those who weren't part of their formulation.

Real vision develops organically. It is not only a clear picture of the best the organisation can be, but it is also deeply felt by everyone involved with the organisation. It involves not only what we want to achieve (typically part of the mission of the organisation), but also what our relationships with one another look like while we're achieving it.

As we discussed in the introduction, the roadmap consists of five steps: Awareness, Exploration and Engagement, Alignment, Commitment, and Acculturate. Client organisations come to us at all different stages of this process, but in an ideal scenario, each of these steps builds on the previous one. It is much easier to explore and engage effectively with the people in your organisation once you are really aware of what is going on. It's hard to bring people into alignment with the organisation's values until you have engaged them, and you will have difficulty connecting meaningfully with people who aren't aligned. And naturally, each of the first four steps is vital to making high performing behaviours part of your organisation's culture.

When you are in the awareness phase, you want to be sure that you are gathering information with the mind-set that you will be moving into the phase of exploration and engagement. During this phase, you will learn about the relationships between people and departments as well as the aspirations of the individuals within the organisation. These may not be exactly the same as the vision for the organisation, but the goal is for those aspirations to be compatible with, and to contribute to, what the organisation wants to achieve. For an organisation to reach its full potential, every employee needs to be empowered to fulfil his or her full potential. This means that they should feel heard, resourced and given opportunities for growth.

The goal of the awareness phase is to uncover the good, the bad and the ugly. You want to learn all you can about the untapped potential of your employees, but you may also uncover some toxic behaviours and dysfunction. All of that is to be expected: no organisation is perfect; just as no human being is perfect. But every organisation can grow and improve, once you become aware of where it really is.

The Alternative to Awareness

Awareness is not inevitable or automatic. Everyone has to deal with reality, but not everyone chooses to do so by facing it head on. For centuries, the Qing Dynasty in China resisted forces of modernisation, believing instead that things could remain as they had been. Japan, by contrast, raced to modernise on its own terms rather than be bullied by the West. When the automobile was invented and mass-produced, some wagon wheel makers learned how to make products for cars while others became obsolete. Many organisations choose to hide from what is really going on in the market or within the organisation itself.

At this stage we are going to assume that your business has the right products, right services and you are in the right market.

Becoming more aware of where your organisation is can be very painful, but it is the vital first step to move an organisation forward. In 2015, Harry took over the regional operations for a huge multi-national transportation company. Excited about his new position, Harry quickly discovered that the branch of the company he was leading was rather immature. The branch lacked structure, and the management team had been put together more by seniority than by leadership ability.

Charged with transitioning the company to be performing at a higher level, Harry soon realised that it needed more than a change in the organisational chart. He concluded that the culture of the organisation itself needed a fundamental transformation. This is often the case: Executive teams frequently recommend more superficial transitions when much deeper change is needed.

Harry came to this conclusion as he became truly aware of what was really going on. He could have simply begun implementing a new management structure as he was told to, but he knew the organisation required something much more than that. He realised that his employees had an "every man for himself" mentality. There was no communication or trust between management and staff and very little transparency.

This reality didn't just make the corporate environment unpleasant; it made it exceedingly inefficient. People showed up to work, and in most cases they didn't really know how their jobs fit with the overall purpose of the company. They performed tasks mechanically, never asking for clarity or direction, and in some cases they had been doing things this way for 10 or 12 years. In response to this realisation, Harry called us, and together we were able to help him build a much more productive culture following the 5 Step Roadmap to Acculturate.

What's Driving Your Organisation?

In 2015, more than 600 students were expelled from schools in the Indian state of Bihar when they were caught cheating on their high school final exams. The same year, eight teachers and administrators in the American city of Atlanta were sentenced to prison for altering students' answers to inflate their performance on standardised tests. In both of these cases, if you had asked the leaders of those schools what the values of the organisation were, their answers would undoubtedly have included ideas like honesty, hard work, and educating young minds. Yet those were not the values driving the behaviour of the Indian students and the American teachers.

Like vision statements, the values of an organisation are too often devised at an exclusive meeting with little thought given to how they will actually be cultivated and applied. If transforming an organisation were as simple as gathering leaders and formulating a list of "company values," every organisation in the world would be functioning at its optimal capacity. But unfortunately, putting a list of values up on a wall or in a mass email does not automatically change the way that people behave. The core values of an organisation are what drive the behaviours of the employees. They may or may not be what is actually written down on paper.

There are often dishonest individuals who cheat or game the system when they think they can get away with it. But the scandals in Bihar and Atlanta were distinct in that the cheating had become so widespread that it had become part of the culture of the organisations. The score on the examinations, not the shaping of young minds or the gaining of knowledge, was driving the behaviour.

A huge part of the awareness stage is determining what values are actually driving your organisation. If you don't like what you see, then this journey is a must for you and your leadership team. Ideally, the core values of a company should be articulated and demonstrated clearly by leadership, and employees should feel a sense of ownership. The organisation will also need a strategy and system to ensure the core values are honoured through, hiring, holding people accountable, incentives and consequences including firing.

Polarity is not unlike the problem of cheating in schools: it can start very small, and if you catch it in its infancy you can avoid its spread. If it has become widespread, however, it will take longer to uproot and replace.

Refer to the exercise at the end of this chapter to gain insight as to what behaviours are driving your organisation.

Getting There is Half the Fun

Becoming aware of both the state of the relationships in your organisation and the values that are driving behaviour can seem like an overwhelming task. It is also easy to feel discouraged when we discover disappointing or distressing realities. Like a long car or plane ride, however, the journey is not nearly so bad if you approach it with positive intent.

Each step of the roadmap is both an art and a science. There are certain guidelines you must follow to connect with people, but there is an intuition you must develop to make those connections truly meaningful. No leader begins his or her career with perfect command of every step; but with the right support and commitment to the process, anyone can master them.

State of The Relationships in Your Organisation?

Purpose: The purpose of this exercise is to gain awareness of relationships, employee aspirations, employee alignment to the organisation's aspirations and how much of their individual potential is being utilised.

Spend 15 minutes in a common area of your organisation (lobby, canteen etc.) being curious of everyone in the place. Without actually talking to anyone, be curious by asking yourself the following questions:

1. How are employees interacting with each other?
2. How are employees interacting with your customers?
3. What are their expressions?
4. How are they carrying themselves (body posture)?
5. How are they reacting to your presence?
6. What else is going on?

At the end of these 15 minutes capture your observations. Then spend some time over the coming days with 3 – 5 (or more) individuals from different parts from the organisation (preferably those who you are unfamiliar with), asking him or her the following questions and see what you discover.

1.   What is important to you?

2.   What do you enjoy most about your work day?

3.   What are your dreams?

4.   What empowers you?

5.   What is holding you back?

6.   What are you missing in your work life?

7.   What's important to you outside the office?

8.   What part of your role fulfils you most?

9.   What motivates you towards success?

10. What recognition do you like best?

11. What is your unique talent?

12. How would you describe your relationship at work?

Now ask yourself the following questions to reveal what behaviours are driving your organisation?

1.   How does this person respond to you when you are curious?

2.   What did you learn about being curious?

3.   What behaviours are driving performance?

4.   What company values are being honoured? Or not honoured?

5.   How do you want to use this information in your organisation?

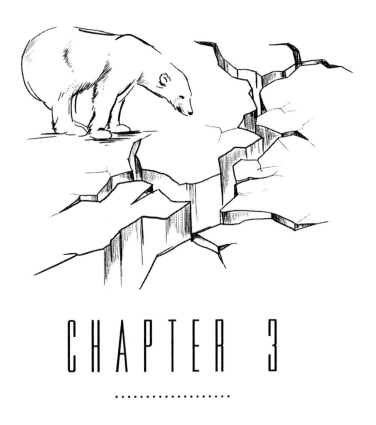

CHAPTER 3

. . . .

Awareness of Your ICE™

The Napoleonic Wars raged in Europe for over a decade, but the Emperor's greatest victory arguably came in the Battle of Austerlitz in December of 1805. Despite his fabled military prowess, the Little General owed much of his battlefield success that day to a surprising ally.

When the Allied forces opposing Napoleon began to retreat, legend has it that thousands of soldiers fell through cracks and fissures in the frozen ponds they had to cross with their cannons. The deadly cold water claimed not only the men's lives, but countless Russian artillery pieces as well.

Now if just one or two men had run over those icy surfaces, they would probably have been fine. But the combination of a large army and heavy cannons proved far too much for the ice to withstand, and tragedy followed.

The same is true of the ICE™ of your organisation that houses all those polar bears and penguins. It may be strong enough to handle the day-to-day traffic, but how will it hold up during a major transition or if a crisis strikes? Is it smooth and solid, allowing everyone to thrive? Or is it cracking, melting or even breaking apart? This chapter will help you find the answer.

Genuine Curiosity and an Open Mind

The ICE™ of an organisation is its Infrastructure, Consciousness and Eco-Wisdom™. These three areas form the environment of your organisational culture and determine its health and productivity. In a diverse organisation housing multiple personalities like the diversity of: polar bears, penguins, arctic hares and leopard seals - the strength of the ICE™ becomes even more important.

We are frequently requested to help organisations manage major transitions, but these don't always occur because things are going wrong. The amazing thing is that the same process of transformation required to transform a polarised company into an aligned organisation will also help you take any business through different stages of growth and development.

Most diverse organisations begin as homogenous associations and then grow to become more varied. As we'll continue to see throughout this book, the internal adjustments that strengthen your ICE™ and help keep polar bears and penguins engaged and aligned together will also improve your business results in the long run.

Assessing your ICE™ is not a simple task list that you check off one by one. It requires genuine curiosity to investigate the relationships, behaviours and skills of the people in your organisation and ask not only "What is going on?" but also "Why is this going on?" For example, it's fairly easy to pull up the resumes of every employee and determine everyone's work history and highest level of education. But it takes genuine curiosity to uncover hidden or underutilised gifts and abilities that could benefit the organisation right now.

One of the easiest mistakes to make while assessing your ICE™ is to allow unspoken or unexamined assumptions to guide your inquiry. Like a detective, you must approach the investigation with an open mind. This requires setting aside preconceived ideas and staying humble about what you think you already understand. Some leaders feel the need to prove to everyone that they know everything, but secure leaders are comfortable not knowing and taking the time to find out.

Assessing your ICE™ is ultimately about owning whatever and wherever your organisation is. It is about uncovering what is going well, what is going okay and what is silently destroying souls. Many leaders do find it helpful to employ an outsider to survey employees, take them through ICE™ diagnosing exercises, and offer a fresh perspective and opinion afterwards. These exercises are often useful for making employees feel valued and heard and can help uncover and diagnose any hidden tension or unrest. But whether you do it yourself or bring in specialists for assistance, it is important to understand well the different components of your ICE™.

Infrastructure

Decades ago, what we typically call corporate infrastructure was exceedingly simple: in most organisations, it probably consisted of a phone system and some typewriters. Today, even medium sized organisations may have a landline telephone system, a mobile phone system, multiple servers, a corporate wired LAN, wireless LAN, a mobile Wi-Fi network and so on. But when we are assessing the infrastructure portion of our ICE™, we are looking at more than just the configuration of these objects and services.

The culture of a country or city is reflected in its peoples' rituals and customs. The cultural infrastructure of an organisation is reflected in the work routines and habits of its employees. What do employees do when they have a question about their job? How do they handle a problem with a customer or an altercation with a co-worker? What about when they have a new idea or a suggestion? How are they rewarded, acknowledged, and celebrated? What are the processes for growth? How does the ethnic diversity either enhance or inhibit each individual's self-expression?

The infrastructure of an organisation is far more than just the list of all the organisational equipment or even the organisational chart depicting the corporate hierarchy.

It is the channels through which authority, responsibility and communication flow. Diverse organisations face particular challenges in this regard. Particularly, differing ethnicities and belief systems can create an environment where similar actions have different meanings and in turn may be unintentionally and easily misunderstood. Like in the Malcolm Gladwell's book Outliers, he gives the example of Korean Airlines flight 801 that crashed. He noted that when the first officer made comments about the weather, he was trying to tell the captain that the weather conditions were dangerous. When he commented on how much he appreciated having weather radar in the cockpit, he meant to suggest that the captain take a look at the radar. Korea's culture is one in which the listener is expected to pick up on subtle cues like this. But the captain was tired, and didn't hear what his first officer was trying to tell him. This failure of communication caused the plane crash.

Korean social norms had a direct effect on what happened in this cockpit. Korean speech tends to put a great deal of interpretive responsibility on the listener. Speakers are not blunt, because they usually don't have to be. The listener will pick up on subtle cues and grasp their meaning without the speaker ever having to say what he means directly. But when the listener is a captain in an airplane, when he is tired and multitasking, this cultural trend becomes dangerous, and in this case led to a crash.

Sometimes the reality of how decisions are made and information is communicated on a day-to-day basis looks more like a bowl of spaghetti than the chart in the corporate handbook. Smooth and effective communication can be particularly challenging when employees bring different sets of preconceived ideas and expectations to the table, which contribute to polarisation.

A healthy infrastructure must strike the delicate balance between the primacy of the vision of the organisation and the importance of each individual within it. Are the employees of your company truly aligned with the vision? Do they believe they are an important part of bringing that vision to pass? Many of us are subconsciously conditioned to believe that work is a zero-sum game—that the rank and file employee is told to serve the organisation, when it seems as though the organisation serves only the needs of its leaders. To teach everyone that we can work together for outcomes that are truly win-win often involves a fundamental transformation of the mind-set of all involved.

Often, whatever authority and responsibility structure exists on paper, the employees do not necessarily know how they apply to their everyday challenges and ideas. If you discover signs of confusion, lack of cooperation, and low morale, these are symptoms of the weakening of the "I" in your ICE™. The weak areas of the "I" are often the result of well-intentioned ideas and strategies that were initiated when the organisation was initially formed, was smaller or was in a different stage of development. Your organisation may have evolved financially, but not emotionally or culturally. The old ICE™ is no longer solid enough to handle the increased weight or changing business environment. The organisation needs to carve the ICE™ to allow the appropriate communication based on the employees' needs to grow personally while growing the business. Not allowing the natural shifting and movement within the organisation will create stagnation, resistance, misalignment and toxicity. Toxic behaviours—covered in more detail in the upcoming chapters—come from two major places: toxic people, or decent people who do not have a productive or healthy way to voice their concerns or thoughts. A healthy infrastructure with sound leadership that constantly seeks feedback is like an immune system that is able to bring toxic behaviours to the surface. Ultimately, the goal is to take the circumstance that created the toxicity and change it into an opportunity for increased awareness and alignment with the organisational objectives.

Corporate infrastructure is most often evaluated for being efficient, and as previously noted, efficiency is important. However, the infrastructure that gets everything done quickly may not be maximising the potential of the organisation. An organisation with a set way for the employees to give feedback on the business processes will have a decided competitive advantage, as we'll discuss below.

Consciousness

Some individuals will maliciously and intentionally undermine the performance of an organisation or a department, but most of the time the harm done to the culture of an organisation is completely unintentional. The "C" in ICE™ is the consciousness of the organisation. How aware are individuals of how their words and actions affect others and the performance of the organisation as a whole? How does that awareness affect their behaviour?

The occasional unintended misunderstanding is unavoidable. The ICE™ is weakened when the consciousness of an organisation is so dull that misunderstandings and offenses become the norm. This is what ultimately polarises a company: people divide into factions, not because they necessarily want to, but because they feel they have to in order to survive psychologically.

A large part of consciousness is associated with emotional intelligence. We can observe that some organisations are more emotionally intelligent than others, but an organisation will only be as strong and skilled as its employees and particularly its leadership. These factors are just as important to consider when building a leadership team as sales numbers and seniority. In fact, one of the biggest issues that we are often brought in to address is basic emotional clumsiness, which is magnified within a diverse population. Fortunately, with the right information and tools, emotional intelligence can be developed and improved.

The consciousness of an organisation will never be greater than the consciousness of each individual within it. It is easy to interpret such a statement as an accusation of fault, but in reality it is quite empowering. If we all have the power to make a valuable contribution to the organisation then our words and actions have the power to affect it for good or bad. Consciousness is really about stewarding that power well.

The more developed the consciousness of an organisation, the more individuals will respect and appreciate each other's differences. Leaders must first demonstrate the kind of consciousness they want to see in their organisation by effective listening. This is the only way to encourage people to take the kind of risks necessary to get the full benefit of the wisdom housed in the organisation and nipping toxic behaviours in the bud. We want people to feel comfortable, not only becoming aware of themselves and how what they do affects others, but we also want them to feel comfortable communicating what they learn and challenging the status quo. When they feel that they can do that at any time within appropriate, productive parameters, then we begin to see the sustainable change we want. That enables the organisation to continue to grow and adjust with the times rather than remaining stagnant.

Eco-Wisdom™

Every species of animal has adapted to thrive in a particular ecosystem. This "Eco-Wisdom™" represents hundreds of thousands or even millions of years of accumulated information about how to interact with and thrive within the environment around them. Human culture is quite similar; people learn from birth how to interpret and respond to subtle facial expressions and all sorts of non-verbal cues. Early in life, we reach the point where we are able to formulate subtle complex responses to a variety of stimuli without even thinking.

Diverse organisations have a tremendous, often untapped, advantage when it comes to Eco-Wisdom™. Instead of two hundred employees who all understand how to interact with, manage and market to the inhabitants of one narrow region of one country, diverse organisations possess within them the potential to reach customers and markets all over the world.

The Eco-Wisdom™ of an organisation can be even greater than the sum of the wisdom of each individual when each is able to share with and learn from others. Harnessing this resource in a diverse company can produce teams of individuals who are uniquely adaptable to all different kinds of situations and clientele. But it takes a truly supportive environment to foster this kind of development. Leaders who are able to engage with their employees and make the process fun, will encourage the kind of creativity and innovation that can ultimately drive the organisation far ahead of the competition.

How well is your organisation utilising its Eco-Wisdom™? Do employees have opportunities for personal and professional growth? These are essential to releasing the untapped potential of the people you already have. Taking the time and effort to ensure all employees are growing and learning will also greatly increase their investment in the vision of the company. Employees who feel valued for their contribution will see their jobs as part of the big-picture goals of the company, instead of just a mundane task list.

Strengthening the ICE™

Bringing our products and services to market is a daily journey, just like commuting to work. If I have a ten mile drive to make each morning and evening, I can choose to obey the traffic laws and drive courteously, or I can be aggressive and obnoxious, cutting off multiple drivers and narrowly avoiding accidents. If I judge my commute strictly by whether or not I get to work, both ways work equally well. But both ways are not equal, and in the long run, the second way is much more likely to raise my blood pressure, get me arrested or even get me killed.

If we judge the organisations we build solely by their profits, we can tolerate dangerously thin ICE™, not worrying about how many bodies may be slipping through as long as they remain beneath the surface. On the other hand, if we take the time to assess and strengthen our ICE™, we will not only see healthy profits in the now, but for years down the road.

Even if everything in your organisation is going well, periodic, proactive ICE™ checks are highly recommended. Assessing your ICE™ requires effort and a shift in focus, but it doesn't necessarily have to take extra time. It doesn't actually take that much longer to have a meaningful conversation than it does to have a superficial one.

Strengthening your ICE™ is not a quick fix. It is a fundamental transformation in the very foundation of your organisation. It is an exciting and gratifying process, which you will find completely worth the effort in the end.

Become aware of the condition of your ICE™ by taking the "Get a feel for your ICE™" assessment at the end of this chapter. You can also engage in a more detailed annual assessment using the Gallup Q12 Employee Engagement Survey which can be self-administered.

The Q12 doesn't ask a lot of questions, it asks the right ones. Gallup's 12 questions accurately measure what matters most to your employees. Keeping your goals in sight, the survey results tie directly to outcomes such as productivity, profitability, and employee retention and turnover.

The 12 questions are:

1. I know what is expected of me at work. (I)

2. At work, my opinions seem to count. (C)

3. I have the materials and equipment I need to do my work right. (I)

4. The mission or purpose of my company makes me feel job is important. (I)

5. At work, I have the opportunity to do what I do best every day. (E)

6. My associates or fellow employees are committed to doing quality work. (I)

7. In the last seven days, I have received recognition or praise for doing good work. (C)

8. I have a best friend at work. (I)

9. My supervisor, or someone at work, seems to care about me as a person. (C)

10. In the last six months, someone at work has talked to me about my progress. (E)

11. There is someone at work who encourages my development. (E)

12. This last year, I have had opportunities at work to learn and grow. (E)

The I, C and E in brackets above, refer to how this survey assesses your ICE™.

Get A Feel For Your ICE™

The ICE™ refers to the Infrastructure Consciousness Eco-Wisdom™ of your organisation. On the next page, ask each member of your leadership team to rank your organisation on a scale of 1 to 5 (where 1 is weak and 5 is strong)

Infrastructure

#	QUESTION	Rank 1-5
1	Every employee knows what is expected of him or her in their role.	
2	All of our employees are capable of performing their role well.	
3	All of our employees have all the information to do their job right/well.	
4	All employee's voices are heard from all diverse groups.	
5	All employees understand how they contribute to the purpose/vision of the organisation every day.	
6	All employee live our company core values.	
7	Our company seeks feedback from our employees on how to improve business processes.	

Consciousness

#	QUESTION	Rank 1-5
8	All leaders demonstrate the kind of consciousness they want to see in the organisation through effectively listening.	
9	During challenging situations, leaders are aware of their emotions/tone, and keep the conversation appropriate.	
10	Leaders manage their emotions; emotions don't manage them.	
11	Leaders respond effectively in a variety of work situations.	
12	Leaders have the ability to read and interpret other people's non-verbal behaviour.	
13	Leaders put their momentary needs on hold to pursue larger more important goals.	
14	Leaders consider issues from others point of view so they can more effectively engage.	

Eco-Wisdom™

#	QUESTION	Rank 1-5
15	Our workplace is positive and productive.	
16	All employees have the opportunity for both professional and personal growth.	
17	Employees' contributions are valued through effective recognition and reward systems.	
18	Our company has healthy and trusting relationships at all levels.	
19	Our company culture encourages our employees to continuously learn and grow.	
20	Our company encourages the sharing of best practices.	

Total number of each ranking:

x1	x2	x3	x4	x5

Multiply by the number above:

Add all five numbers to determine the percentage score that reflects the current state of your ICE™.

%

80%+ = Strong ICE™ that can withstand the weight

60% - 80 % = Depending on the weight you could be at risk

less than 60% = I hope you know how to survive in icy cold waters!

STEP 2

. . . .

EXPLORATION & ENGAGEMENT

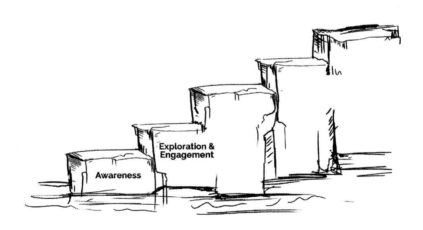

CHAPTER 4

· · · · · · · · · · · · · · · · · ·

Rules of Engagement

On December 14, 1911, Roald Amundsen and his team of Norwegian **explorers** became the first human beings to reach the South Pole. A treacherous journey plagued by bad weather, the men were able to achieve their goal by careful preparation, good equipment, appropriate clothing, a simple primary task, an understanding of dogs and their handling, and the effective use of skis. In contrast to the misfortunes of Robert Falcon Scott's team, Amundsen's trek proved relatively smooth and uneventful. The utilisation of sled dogs was an example of proper planning—the sled dogs fared much better in the

Antarctic conditions than the Siberian ponies the rival British team used with less success.

Once you've become more aware of what is going on in your organisation, it's time to get out there and start exploring the ICE™ by engaging with those polar bears and penguins. Although you're less likely than Amundsen to suffer from frostbite along the way (or maybe not!), your journey will still require some preparation and supplies. And just like no one thought the journey to the South Pole would be easy, it's best to give up the hope of a "quick fix" from the beginning and settle in for the long haul. A friendly reminder of one of the guiding principles—Be Committed.

Relationship Design

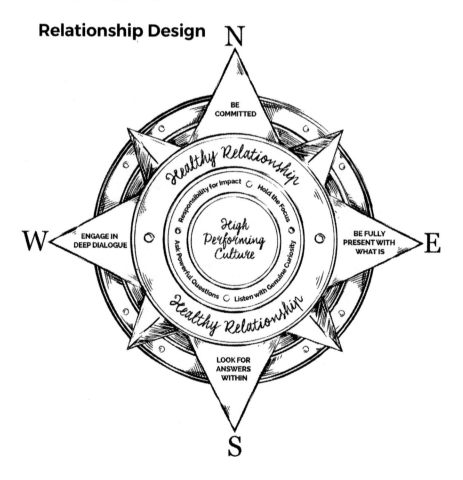

The first step to exploration and engagement is to set the parameters for the relationship moving forward.

In most organisations, the working relationship between employees, management and executives is not spelled out, so people make assumptions. These assumptions may or may not be accurate, and the existing relationship is rarely as functional as it could be. Regardless of the specifics, an undefined or loosely defined relationship will be tested in a diverse organisation, particularly when a crisis or a transition hits.

Before engaging, leaders must assess the state of those relationships and redesign them if necessary. Do people feel respected and valued? Do they know what to do when they feel upset or offended? What about when they have a good idea or a suggestion? Keep in mind during the exploration and engagement phase that most people just want to feel that they are being seen and heard. This may look and feel different in different cultures, but the human need is ultimately the same.

If the relationship isn't designed correctly from the beginning, the rest of the process will not be as effective as it could be. Relationship design is almost like a roommate agreement or even marriage vows: the ground rules for how we are going to conduct ourselves and treat each other as we move forward together. In a healthy relationship design, these ground rules will include topics like openness, honesty and non-judgmental listening. It will also involve an honest assessment about what is going wrong in the relationship: where is trust being violated? Which appropriate boundaries are being honoured and which ones are being disrespected?

Rule #1 - Responsibility for Impact

Everyone involved must feel confident that they can be transparent and authentic about their thoughts and feelings without negative consequences. They should feel comfortable sharing openly without feeling the need to defend themselves. This starts with the leadership team. Leaders must take responsibility for their impact and manage it accordingly to bring out the best for those in relationship with them. In other words, they must understand how they are perceived by polar bears, penguins, artic hares and the leopard seals.

Rule #2 - Holding the Focus

Designing these kinds of relationships is not complicated but it does have to be intentional and precise. The challenge facing diverse organisations is to allow all employees to be themselves while "holding the focus" on the organisations purpose and vision. The good news is, that when the relationship is intentionally designed and leaders stay focused on the purpose and vision, the ICE™ will remain strong in the face of challenges.

Keep in mind that designing the relationship is not a one-time event. It is something that you will come back to over and over again during the transformation journey and even beyond as the organisation faces new challenges and changes. As Daniel Goleman —author of *Emotional Intelligence and Social Intelligence*—clearly articulates, "Understanding is only part of a relationship; it is what you do with it that really matters".

Rule #3 - Ask Powerful Questions

The way to find out what is really going on is to ask **powerful questions,** which support the guiding principle of "deep dialogue". These questions are like the sled dogs in your arctic exploration: they will take you where you need to go. One of the greatest challenges in a diverse organisation is the fact that different cultures have very different understandings about what is socially acceptable to share. Polar bears might ask a woman very directly about her recent weight gain, while penguins would never dream of bringing it up. On the other hand, polar bears might be very uncomfortable with direct questioning regarding a family matter, while penguins might chat freely about a brother's divorce or a mother's hospitalisation.

Asking powerful questions requires a level of emotional intelligence, but that can be learned and developed by leaders. When asking powerful questions, it's important to be willing to gently bend a few polar bear and penguin taboos with the goal of forging a new workplace culture where everyone can be open about the things that are important to the success of the organisation as well as to the individual. This can be done in a way that isn't perceived as rude but rather as liberating: giving people permission to express how they really feel.

One of the most powerful ways to engage your polar bears, penguins, artic hares and leopard seals is to ask them to complete this sentence:

"I work best when…"

This is an open-ended inquiry that gently encourages the respondents to consider what they need in order to be productive. What do they need in order to do their job well? The flip side of the question indirectly forces the respondent to consider which aspects of productivity are his or her own responsibilities. If I have what I need, what should I be producing? Other powerful questions include:

What is working well for you right now?

What is keeping you awake at night?

If you could change just one thing about work, what would it be?

What are relationships like in the workplace right now for you?

Do you have friends there?

How excited are you to get up in the morning and come to work?

Sometimes questions with calibrated answers can help employees express their feelings more accurately:

On a scale of 1-10, how fulfilled are you in your job right now?"

What would a 10 look like for you?

Not all powerful questions have to come in response to a crisis or even a challenge. Some of the best questions to ask on an ongoing basis include:

What can we improve?

How can we grow?

The key to these kinds of powerful questions is to ask them in a spirit of genuine curiosity. Listeners will sense this and respond with accurate, honest descriptions of what they feel, not justifications for what they think or do. Judgement will be received with defensiveness, but curiosity will often be received with genuine helpfulness and openness.

For an extensive list of powerful questions to assist you in this exploration please refer to the exercise at the end of this chapter.

Rule #4 - Listen with Genuine Curiosity

Powerful questions are all well and good. However, if the leader is not prepared to listen without interrupting the speaker with his or her own thoughts and feelings, the interaction may do more harm than good.

It takes practice to know what a person is feeling and how this affects his or her behaviour in the workplace. When asking powerful questions, it is very important to also pay attention to the other person's body language, tone and volume of voice and speed of movement, known as level 2 of listening.

We worked with a media company that brought us in to help them develop their vision, mission and values. As we began exploring and engaging, we found that there were many different perspectives regarding what the culture of the company was really like. When we spoke with the CEO, he was confident that they had a great workplace environment. It was easy to see why he felt that way: revenues were fine and he wasn't personally aware of anyone being discontent—this organisation scored 67% in the ICE™ assessment.

We encouraged him to get curious, and he allowed us to ask his employees powerful questions. As soon as we began the process, we immediately sensed that there were some important things not being said. Everything from people's facial expressions and body language to the heaviness of the air the room was telling us that there was something that needed to come out. So we asked, "What is it that isn't being said right now?"

To be fully present with what is (another reminder of how important our guiding principles are), we waited in silence. We knew the answers were in the room and we were committed to take as much time as required to be able to engage in deep dialogue. To facilitate deep dialogue effectively, you have to be okay with some extended awkward silences. It's very tempting for leaders to fill those silences by sharing their own thoughts, insights and ideas. After all, that's what most leaders like to do. But talking to fill the silences is effectively denying a voice the right to be heard. To explore and engage effectively, you sometimes need to allow enough time for the truth to come out.

When the answers finally began to come, we didn't shut the discussion down or try to move on. We asked another one of our favourite powerful questions: "What else?" What else is bothering you? What else have you wanted to say but haven't? This kind of questioning and listening treats the entire exercise as a truly exploratory mission, not a task to be completed and checked off the list.

Listening well is powerful. Over and over, we have observed that if the facilitators and leaders are committed to listening well during the explore and engagement phase, the atmosphere of the room softens and people open up. The dialogue gets deeper and lasting trust is built.

Organisations all across the world face different circumstances and market conditions. But exploration and engagement exercises enable you to rise above the circumstances and evaluate the relationships on your team. When those relationships are strong, it doesn't matter what outside factors show up. You may have had a merger or acquisition or the country may be rife with civil unrest. Whether you land the biggest client or lose a crucial deal, your team will be ready to work through it together.

If listening well is an area of opportunity for you please refer to the levels of listening exercises at the end of this chapter to strengthen this skill in you and your team.

When important concerns or grievances are left unsaid they become more than a source of discontentment. They can become a breeding ground for toxic behaviours. No matter how proactive you are, there is a good chance that you will encounter some of these during your exploration and engagement phase. In the next chapter, we'll cover how to identify toxic behaviours and dispose of them effectively.

Now take some time to complete the Relationship Design— Exploration exercise at the end of this chapter with your leadership team before you explore and engage with the entire organisation.

Relationship Design Exploration

This tool is about taking responsibility for relationships within your leadership team and/or functional team that could be healthier and thus more productive.

The designing of a relationship can happen at any time and will tend to shift over time and need to be revisited regularly. Whether you intentionally design or not, designing is happening, so you may as well be intentional about it! Relationships are custom-designed to meet the particular needs of the individual(s)/team(s) involved. All parties are intimately involved in designing the relationship that will be most beneficial for the greater good.

The steps:

Do the quick self-assessment on the next page in the context of relationships within the leadership team. This assessment can be performed on any relationship of two or more people.

Instructions:

1. Please evaluate the statements honestly and objectively. Don't agonise over your responses—your initial "gut feel" is usually best.

2. Use the scale below to indicate how each statement applies to the relationship your are assessing.

3. Use the full range of the 1—5 scale

2—Rarely 3—Sometimes 4—Usually 5—Always

#	STATEMENT	Rate 1-5
1	We are comfortable openly sharing without the need to defend.	
2	We take responsibility for our impact on one another.	
3	We can be ourselves without judgement or repercussions.	
4	We hold the focus on our organisation's mission and vision under all circumstances.	
5	We are open about things that are important to the success of our organisation, no matter how controversial it is.	
6	We are committed to taking as much time as possible to engage in deep dialogue.	
7	We take time to celebrate the successes of the team and individuals within it.	
8	We listen to each other with genuine curiosity.	

Total score:

SCORE	STRENGTH OF THE RELATIONSHIP
HIGH (30 AND ABOVE)	You have created an environment where vulnerability and openness for the betterment of the organisation are a norm.
MEDIUM (26 TO 29)	You need to get more comfortable in embracing the rules of engagement.
LOW (25 AND BELOW)	Your relationship lacks necessary levels of openness and vulnerability and keep reading the book!

If your assessment is in the "Low" or "Medium" score then follow the steps on the following page.

Step 1

Recognise the relationship is not as good as it could

Some relationships will only require a minor adjustment. C ..

relationships may be dysfunctional or awkward.

Step 2

Spot the signs of an unhealthy relationship. This is where either party displays or repeatedly feels; hostility, discomfort, anger, avoidance, contempt, fear, criticism etc. And then get into conversation by asking the following questions:

- *What would be possible if this relationship was better?*
- *Look at the possibility of creating ground rules with this person.*
- *What are you no longer prepared to tolerate?*
- *When are you willing to compromise?*
- *What are the consequences if the boundaries are crossed?*

Step 3

Remember that designing relationships goes both ways. The idea is to have a conversation and agree on as many things as possible, which could include:

- *How to work with each other when not agreeing?*
- *How we deal with failure?*
- *How do we communicate when tempers flare?*
- *How can I best let you know if you have crossed a boundary?*

Powerful Questions For Exploration & Engagement

Powerful leaders ask powerful questions, taking the other to a place of exploration. The qualities of powerful questions are:

1. Open-ended—beginning with "what" or "how", cannot be answered with yes or no.

2. Lead to greater creativity and insight.

3. Invite introspection.

4. Short in length—typically 7 words or less.

5. Only one question at a time—avoid stacking on top of another.

Some Examples of Powerful Questions*:

Options

What are the possibilities?

If you had your choice, what would you do?

What are possible solutions that you see?

Evaluation

What do you make of all of this?

What do you think? (is best?)

How do you see it?

How do you feel about it?

Contextual

What led up to _____?

What have you tried so far?

What do you make of it all?

Clarification

What do you mean?

What seems to confuse you?

Explanation

What was it like?

What happened?

Then what?

Valuation

How does this fit with the organisation's core values?

How does this fit with the organisation's purpose?

What do you think?

Searching

What are the brainstorm ideas you have?

What are the other angles you can think of?

Sample

For instance?

Like what?

Such as?

Expansion

What else?

What other ideas do you have?

Imaginary

If you could redo what you did, what would you do differently?

What would you have done?

How else could this have been handled?

Identification

What seems to be the trouble?

What seems to be the main obstacle?

What is getting in your way?

What are the concerns you have?

Implementation

What will you have to do to get the job done?

What support do you need to accomplish _____?

What will you do?

By when will you do it?

Information

What information do you need before you decide?

What do you know about it now?

How do you suggest we can find out more about it?

Assimilation

How do you explain this?

What is the lesson/learning?

How would you pull all this together?

Participation

What was your part in this?

How do you fit into the picture?

What are you responsible for?

New beginning

If you had free choice in the matter, what would you do?

If the same thing came up again, what would you do?

If we could wipe the slate clean, what would you do?

If you had it to do over again, what would you do?

Results

What do you want?

What is your desired outcome?

If you got this result, what would you have?

How will you know you have received/reached it?

Forecasting

What do you plan to do about it?

What is your game plan?

What kind of plan do you need to create?

How do you suppose you could improve the situation?

Predictions

How do you suppose it will all work out?

What will that get you?

Where will this lead?

What are the chances of success?

Relativity

If you do this, how will it affect _____?

How does this affect the whole picture?

What else do you need to take into consideration?

Taking Action

What action will you take? And after that?

What will you do? When?

Where do you go from here? When will you do that?

What are your next steps? By when?

Summary

How is this working? How is this going?

How would you describe this?

What do you think this all amounts to?

How would you summarise the work/effort so far?

Select the question(s) that you feel will best serve you and the relationship.

*Adapted from the Co-Active Coaching Book by The Coaches Training Institute

Levels of Listening & Self Development Exercise

A good listener is able to move swiftly and consciously between the different levels of listening depending on the situation. The key is awareness of which level you are in, and which level you need to be in to have your desired impact.

Level 1—'Internal Listening'

Listening is necessary in order to make a decision or to make a judgement call. Then it's perfectly fine to allow yourself to be informed by Level 1.

e.g.: Ordering from a menu or choosing the seat to sit in on an aeroplane.

Level 2—'Listening to Understand'

Is necessary when you need to ensure that you are both understood and that you understand the other person. Being able to identify the other person's underlying emotions is an important leadership skill. Respected leaders are good at listening at Level 2.

Level 3—'Global Listening'

Listening is particularly important when you work in a group setting or when you are leading people. Having a sense of what the mood is in your environment will allow you the opportunity to shift it if necessary.

Exercise—Level 1

The objective of this exercise is to listen completely at level 1, focusing entirely on your own thoughts and opinions. Do this exercise with a family member (or partner). Ask them to describe their ideal next holiday destination, including example of things to do, see, experience and places to go while on holiday. As your family member tells the story, your job is to listen to the words and interpret the story entirely from your own wants and desires (perspective). Make frequent comments in which you offer your opinion. Think about how you would organise the trip differently.

What's going on in your head while the other person is talking/sharing? What does this experience remind you of in your work life? When finished, ask each other what it was like to listen and be listened to at level 1.

Exercise—Level 2

Work with your family member on the same story, and this time be curious. Ask questions, clarify and be alert for your partners' values (what's important) as they express the story. Stay completely focused on your family member by listening and responding with empathy, clarification and collaboration.

When finished tell each other what it is like to listen and be listened to at level 2? How was this experience different from level 1? How can this apply in your organisation? What are you committing to do differently?

Exercise—Level 3

Take some time out to visit various departments in your organisation and be a "fly on the wall" as you visit. Your intention is to identify what the "mood" is in the environment. This takes genuine curiosity and consciousness of your own impact as you enter the room/environment. How do the various departments differ from each other? What did you notice? How does this align to the "mood" with the leadership environment? What are you learning about Level 3? What are you confirming?

CHAPTER 5

·················

Getting Rid of Toxic Waste

Anyone who has watched an old building being demolished sees first-hand that is takes much longer to build something than it does to tear it down. We have witnessed civil unrest dismantle the culture of long-standing organisations within the Middle East in a matter of weeks. We have also seen companies lose clients and experience a devastating drop in morale. Other organisations face industry shifts that force radical changes at every level of the organisation. None of these events are within anyone's full control, yet they have a detrimental impact on the employees' motivation and confidence.

Sometimes even positive changes can unearth some unexpected negativity. When we worked with a hotel in a major city in America that had been around for decades, its leadership decided to transition from being a standalone hotel to adopting the banner of an international brand. The people who had worked there for years didn't understand why this was necessary. They didn't see the advantage of making what they perceived as a drastic change, and some of them felt that part of their identity was being taken away.

This example of organisational deterioration may have been unexpected, but the underlying polarity was there all along. During the exploration and engagement phase, you will be uncovering underlying polarity and toxicity. Ideally, you will be able to do this proactively, ahead of any major crisis. But even if you are already experiencing upheaval in your organisation, you can minimise the negative effects by addressing the issues you discover right away.

Just because an organisation is polarised doesn't mean that everything in the organisation is going wrong. It just means that people are more connected to and aware of all the things that are going wrong, rather than all the things that may be going right. During this phase, you will be investigating the sources of toxicity as well as any negative baggage that people have from previous attempts at change. Sometimes you will discover that people feel like they have offered input and suggestions in the past and that no one listened to what they said or nothing was done. Regardless of what you find in your exploration, remember that the productive reaction to any negative indicator is not panic but **genuine curiosity.**

Dealing with POOP™

Both polar bears and penguins produce plenty of poop, and poop is one of those topics that makes everyone uncomfortable. It's messy and smelly but ubiquitous nonetheless. In the exploration and engagement phase, you will uncover your fair share of POOP™, which for the sake of our discussion stands for four things: 1. **Preconceived Ideas** 2. **Obstacles** 3. **Obsessions** and 4. **Prejudices.**

Preconceived Ideas

All of us bring preconceived ideas to work with us, and these tend to vary greatly by culture. Preconceived ideas are not wrong in and of themselves. The problem comes when we fail to recognise and critically examine them.

Preconceived ideas often cover the grey areas of behaviour such as the way we demonstrate courtesy and respect. Polar bears may consider it rude if you fail to bow to a new acquaintance, but penguins may be comfortable kissing someone on the cheek when they first meet. Part of exploring and engaging is uncovering these preconceived ideas and determining where they may be causing unnecessary conflict and polarity.

Take a few quiet moments alone and ask **yourself** the following questions to become aware of your preconceived ideas:

1. What's the image that you hold of this organisation?
2. How do others see the organisation's capabilities?
3. What other ideas, thoughts and feelings do you have about this organisation?
4. What's the image you hold of this team?
5. How do you see their capabilities?
6. What other ideas, thoughts and feelings do you have about this team/organisation?

Obstacles

There are all kinds of obstacles that you may uncover when you begin exploring your organisation. The obstacles in POOP™, however, are the personal challenges that prevent individuals from doing their jobs well and reaching their goals. These can include everything from the attitude they bring to work to any challenges they may face involving fear, anxiety or even depression. Other personal obstacles could include skill or educational deficiencies or other professional needs. Begin cataloguing the obstacles you uncover so that you can strategise how to help individuals overcome them.

Take a few quiet moments alone and ask **yourself** the following questions to become aware of your obstacles:

1. What challenges are getting in the way of people doing their jobs well?

2. What are some of the fears in the organisation?

3. What's not being said?

4. What concerns you the most about...?

5. What is holding your organisation back?

6. What are some of the barriers?

Obsessions

Everyone has different preferences when it comes to their workplace environment. These can include simple things like the temperature in the office, cleanliness of workspaces and common areas, as well as more complicated things, such as how frequently individuals are expected to check in with management on various projects or assignments. Different people have different levels of comfort regarding certain kinds of deadlines, and they react differently when there are changes to a particular project or protocol.

An inclination or a preference becomes an obsession when the person in question is unable to bend on the issue when circumstances require it. Diverse organisations need a certain degree of flexibility from everyone if they are to flourish. Take careful note of any obsessions you uncover during the exploration phase, so that they can be handled directly and sensitively.

Take a few quiet moments alone and ask **yourself** the following questions to become aware of your obsessions:

1. What are you hanging onto?

2. What are you intolerant to?

3. What are you not prepared to let go of?

4. If you could wipe the slate clean what would you do?

5. What's really important for you right now?

6. What's important about that?

7. What are the drivers behind that?

Prejudices

All human beings bring prejudices to the table. These may include assumptions about management, co-workers and even the organisation itself. Most people have been repeatedly told that prejudice is wrong, whether in school or in a business setting. Unfortunately, this has led many to believe they must deny having any prejudices at all, rather than admitting them and examining them critically. Do your best to create a non-judgmental, comfortable space where people can admit their prejudices on their own.

Take a few quiet moments alone and ask **yourself** the following questions to become aware of your prejudices:

1. What have you made up about people on your team?
2. What judgement have you formulated?
3. What are the beliefs around this?
4. What are you tolerating?

The best way to get rid of POOP™ is for each individual to learn to dispose of it properly in the first place! Let us remind you the productive reaction to POOP™ in an organisation is not panic, but genuine curiosity to awaken a hunger for something better—that's what the exploration is all about.

So in this exploration we are going to hear things that can create the environment for judging, defensiveness and the need to explain and justify. We have to remind ourselves of the guiding principles on this journey of **being fully committed, being fully present with what is, engage in deep dialogue and believe that the answers are within.**

Referring back to Daniel Goleman stating that "understanding what is going on is only part of a healthy relationship, it is what you do with it, that really matters". How you respond to your own POOP™ observations and what you hear from others in your organisation in this stage of the journey will be a make or break to the desired transformation. There is no room for judging, repercussions or reprisals. This exploration is done with a spirit of genuine curiosity.

Awareness of Your Emotional Intelligence

We highly recommend that you and your leadership team take the time to explore your readiness for this part of the journey by taking the Emotional Intelligence (EQ) assessment at the end of this chapter to have an awareness of self and your impact on others. Once each leader has completed the EQ assessment we invite you to partake in the Johari Window team building activity also located at the end of this chapter. This activity will provide further insight into the impact you have on others around you. From this exercise, what do you and your leadership team need to commit to whilst maintaining healthy relationships as you navigate this part of the journey?

Emotional management is one of the most difficult skills to master as a leader and in teams because most of the members of any team are not always comfortable managing their emotions publically or discussing emotions in a group setting. It requires a commitment from the leadership team to work together to spot when emotions are steering their progress or lack there of. The goal is to interact effectively with one another when we are in this exploration and engagement phase to ensure that we respond well to difficult situations. Without this, toxic behaviours can creep into this journey, causing a major weather system and devastating damage in its aftermath.

Toxic Behaviours

The Four Horsemen of the Apocalypse is a metaphor depicting the end of times in the New Testament. They describe conquest, war, hunger, and death respectively. Dr. Gottman uses this metaphor to describe communication styles that can predict the end of a relationship.

The first horseman of the apocalypse is **criticism**. Criticising your colleague is different than offering a critique or voicing a complaint! The latter two are about specific issues, whereas the former is a personal attack: it is an attack on your colleague at the core. In effect, you are dismantling his or her whole being when you criticise. E.g. "you are selfish".

The second horseman is **defensiveness**. We've all been defensive. When we feel accused unjustly, we fish for excuses or justifications so that our colleague will back off. Unfortunately, this strategy is almost never successful.

The third horseman is **contempt**. When we communicate in this state, we are truly mean—treating others with disrespect, mocking them with sarcasm, ridicule, name-calling, mimicking, and/or body language such as eye-rolling. The target of contempt is made to feel despised and worthless.

The fourth horseman is **stonewalling**. Stonewalling occurs when the listener withdraws from the interaction. In other words, stonewalling is when one person shuts down and closes himself/herself off from the other. It is a lack of responsiveness to your colleague and the interaction between the two of you. Rather than confronting the POOP™ (which tends to accumulate!) with our colleagues, we make evasive manoeuvres such as tuning out, turning away, acting busy, or engaging in obsessive behaviours. It takes time for the negativity created by the first three horsemen to become overwhelming enough that stonewalling becomes an understandable "out," but when it does, it frequently becomes a habit.

Being able to identify *The Four Horsemen*, which we refer to as the **Four Toxic Behaviours** in this book, is a necessary first step to eliminating them, but this knowledge is not enough. To drive away destructive communication patterns, you must replace them with healthy, productive ones.

So what can you do if you notice yourself participating in or being subjected to criticism, defensiveness, contempt, and/or stonewalling?

1. Learn to make specific complaints & requests rather than criticisms by using the "I, Feel, When, Because" technique.
    EXAMPLE:
    Complaint: I felt scared when you were running late and didn't call me because I thought we had agreed that we would do that for each other."
    VERSUS:
    Criticism: "You never think about how your behaviour is affecting other people. I don't believe you are that forgetful, you're just selfish! You never think of others! You never think of me!"

2. Learn to communicate consciously by speaking to the facts rather than personality.

3. Learn to listen for accuracy, for the core emotions your colleague is expressing and for what your colleague really wants. What you are really listening for is the "hidden request". What is the request that is trying to be made amongst all the noise? Behind every blame and/or criticism there is always a hidden request, we just need to listen for it. The hidden request from the above criticism is "Please can you inform me next time you will be late"?

4. Shift to appreciation (5 positive interactions are necessary to compensate for one negative interaction) "What I appreciate about what I'm hearing is…"
    EXAMPLE:
    "What I'm hearing you say is that you were worried for my safety and I want to thank you for your concern"

5. Claim responsibility.

    EXAMPLE:

    "What can I learn from this?" and "What can I do about it?"

6. Re-write your inner script (notice when you are thinking critical, contemptuous or defensive thoughts; replace thoughts of righteous indignation or innocent victimisation with thoughts of appreciation, and respect that are soothing, validating and more constructive)

7. Practice getting "un-triggered": (allowing your colleagues utterances to be what they really are: just thoughts and puffs of air) and let go of the POOP™, stories, judgments and assumptions that you are making up

Refer to the 4 Toxic Behaviours case study at the end of this chapter for a real life example.

Proper POOP™ Disposal

Ultimately, the purpose of exploring the POOP™ is to awaken a hunger for something better. If we're not improving, we're moving backwards. No marketplace is a static environment. Chances are, your competition is working to get better, and new competitors are arriving on the horizon. If you stand still, you'll be left behind.

> *"Change has never happened this fast before*
> *and it will never be this slow again"*
>
> —Graeme Wood, Author of *Small Data*

These conversations not only suck all the energy out of the room, they also make people feel very uncomfortable. It's important to emphasise that you will not be camping out in this place for long. But these exercises serve a very important purpose. They get everyone's fears out in the open, and they also remind everyone of the cost of doing nothing.

One of the most important exercises you can do with your team is to explore the worst-case scenarios they envision for the company. This is not a pleasant task, and it can't be skipped. To get things rolling, we will often ask people a powerful question like, "What is the worst thing that could happen if we do not address our POOP™ effectively?"

The answers are rarely optimistic. Here are some common responses:

"We'll lose market share."

"Our revenues will drop."

"Downsizing."

"We'll lose brand recognition."

"We'll lose great talent in the organisation."

"No more promotions."

"Pay and bonus cuts."

"No more personal development. No professional development."

Once you get all these doom and gloom scenarios out on the table, you can ask each respondent to calibrate his answer. "On a scale of 1-10, how connected do you feel to what you just described?" This lets you know if these predictions are just lurking in the back of people's minds or if they actually feel discouraged and pessimistic.

The POOP™ is like a sandstorm. You could be in a luxurious skyscraper looking out over the most beautiful city in the world, but during a sandstorm you can't see more than two or three hundred meters in front of you. When we're haunted by the POOP™, we don't see the vision of where the company is headed; we only see what is going on around us right now.

The goal is not to embarrass or humiliate anyone in attendance or meant to be used as an excuse to bash the organisation. Sensitivity (Emotional Intelligence) and a genuine curiosity is typically a very effective approach in forging useful dialogue.

Move to action.

In keeping with the animal theme of "don't beat a dead horse" discuss it and debate but only say what you want to say once. Repeating is politicking.

Once you have surfaced and discussed what the POOP™ is, using the powerful questions at the end of this chapter, as a team everyone must share their thoughts, ideas, concerns and solutions to disposing of the POOP™. Once everyone agrees, or at least can live with the decision, someone needs to take ownership of the disposal! From there, there must be a united front moving forward.

Cleaning up after you have collected all the POOP™ in the room is messy business. It takes time, patience, and heart—as you test emotions and push boundaries. Only by bringing to the surface and deliberating over un-discussables can we ensure our teams operate to their full potential.

Signs of Successful Engagement

Disengagement often begins innocently enough: not bothering to greet co-workers' when they arrive at work, keeping their heads down, looking at their phones instead of making eye contact. If enough people behave that way, over time they begin to wonder if it matters if they're ten minutes late today, or tomorrow or the next day. Ultimately, you are left with employees who take no ownership for their behaviour or productivity.

The sandstorms of POOP™ and discouragement cause people to become disengaged. They can't see all the possibilities the future holds because fear and uncertainty are obscuring their view. But talking about these apprehensions allows people to become aware of the destructive emotions associated with such ideas. They realise that thinking that way—even subconsciously—drains their motivation and energy and causes them to become disengaged and stressed out.

The purpose of your exploration is to engage your polar bears and penguins, not just make them happier. It's important to remember that employees can be happy and engaged or happy and disengaged. Engagement means getting everyone connected (or reconnected) to the purpose and the vision of the company. This means that they see themselves as a vital part of that big picture, and so find meaning in the work they do every day.

To engage your polar bears and penguins, you have to go beyond just listening, to doing something concrete with what you hear. This has short term and long-term implications. In the short term, it means demonstrating that you are serious about change. In the long term, it means demonstrating the consistency and commitment to see the process through to the end.

Not long ago I ate at a new restaurant in London. The décor was elegant and the food excellent, but the service was definitely substandard. I took the time to let the maître d' know, not because I wanted him to reduce my bill, but because I enjoyed the food, and I wanted the restaurant to be successful. Naturally I expected better service the next time I returned, and I received it. If I had gone back and had the same issues as before, I would have assumed the management didn't hear or value what I said.

Now you may find after your explorations that you cannot immediately act on every suggestion that has been made. In those cases you need to speak clearly about the situation. For example, you might say something like, "We've heard that a number of you are not happy that we don't have enough parking spaces. Unfortunately, we aren't able to add more parking right now. What we would like to do is offer sign-up sheets in the break room for those who would like to carpool until the situation is rectified." This isn't a perfect solution, but it lets them know you've heard them and that you are serious about fixing the problem.

Once you've heard the POOP™, it's also tempting to rush to fix as many problems as quickly as possible. The problem with this approach is that you will—by necessity—fix the smallest and most superficial problems to try to address any immediate issues with morale. Some gift cards or time off may be important steps to show that you really have heard what has been said and are taking it seriously. But you cannot stop there. You have to continue on to the bigger issues, building that trust and maintaining the engagement.

It's incredibly encouraging for people to realise that they can make the decision to do something about what they don't like. We recently worked with a media company of about 30 people. Because it was such a small group, we were able to meet with the entire team. We found that every one of them left the meeting with a personal commitment and a sense of empowerment. They saw small steps they could take today to move their organisation towards its goals, but they also recognised that these steps were just the beginning.

Transforming a culture takes time. The goal of engagement is to bring everyone to the short-term commitment to do something today that can help make the organisation better and to the long-term commitment to be an active part of the overall transformation.

Exploration and engagement are not the end of the journey; they are the beginning. If you have completed this phase successfully, your employees are saying to themselves, "They heard us on the parking spaces. Maybe we can trust them with something bigger." This is the beginning of building the trust necessary to bring about the transformation you are looking for. Even more, success means that people don't just believe that their concerns were heard; they see themselves as part of the solution.

The 4 Toxic Behaviours—Case Study*

*"Appreciation is Greater" Case study: (adapted from February 28, 2017, Grace is Greater by Kyle Idleman.

"How difficult is it to push a button on the dishwasher? My vote is "not very," but that isn't the point. What made the whole thing ironic is that I was in the middle of writing a lecture on "happiness." Let me explain…

My wife and I were staying at a condo we'd rented in Florida. We had to check out by 10 a.m. on Friday. Before checkout the renter is asked to do a few things: strip the sheets off the bed, put all the towels in the hallway, take out the trash, then load and start the dishwasher. My wife assigned me dishwasher duty. At about 10:05, an older man and a couple of women walked into the condo, spotted me, and said, "Ummm, we are here to clean. You were supposed to be out of here by 10."

I apologised, thanked them and told them we were headed out the door. We grabbed our stuff and made our way down to the car. Just before we reached it, the guy came out of our room and yelled down to us in the parking lot, "Hey! Thanks a lot for starting the dishwasher. There's only a few things you're asked to do and you couldn't bring yourself to push the button?"

I'd just finished writing a lecture explaining that because we have belief, our circumstances don't have to rob us of joy. So, you might think I would respond humbly. Instead, I thought, Oh, you want to overreact and get sarcastic? I can speak that language. I yelled up at him, "I'm so sorry you had to push that button. I'm sure that had to be exhausting," and then laughed condescendingly. He yelled back at me, with a few more choice words, and I yelled back at him.

The last thing I heard is him calling me "a worthless..." I got in the car and slammed the door. I sat there steaming about how I'd been disrespected. My wife said, "Let's just go." Instead of listening, I said, "Oh, no. That man needs to hear some hard truth." I got out of the car, and then heard my wife tell me, "Say a quick prayer on your way up." I headed up the stairs to confront Mr. "Can't push the button on the dishwasher in the condo but has plenty of energy to yell at me from the third-floor balcony." After the first flight of stairs, I felt convicted and embarrassed. By the second floor I was telling God I was sorry, and almost immediately it was impressed upon me that I needed to apologise and give the man a tip for his extra work. I opened my wallet, to realise I only had a single bill — which was more than I intended to give him. I thought, well, apparently giving the man a tip is not what God wants me to do.

I walked into the condo, and he started yelling again. I sensed a voice inside me saying, One more round!

Even though I didn't feel like it, I said, "I want to apologise. I'm sure it's frustrating to come in and clean up after someone who doesn't do the little things. I'm sorry. I want to give this to you for the extra work you have to do and as a way to say thank you." I held out the money. Almost immediately his eyes welled up with tears. He said,

"Well, I wasn't expecting that," and began to apologise. Now my eyes were filled with tears. I think we both wanted to hug it out, but instead we just shook hands.

I walked back down the steps, not feeling proud of that moment, but instead broken hearted it had reached the point it did. I asked myself, How many similar moments had I forgotten about the wisdom of appreciation and let my pride get in the way?

I wondered: How many times I wanted me to show grace and humility but I was too arrogant and self-righteous? I sat down in the car, teary-eyed. My wife asked, "What happened?" I told her. She patted me on the leg and said with a smile, "Oh, it's so cute. You're growing up.'"

EQ Assessment*—Responsibility for Impact

Emotional intelligence (referred to as EQ) is the ability to be aware of, understand and manage your emotions. Why is EQ important? While intelligence (referred to as IQ) is important, success in life depends more on EQ. Take the assessment below to learn your EQ strengths!

Adapted from the San Diego City College MESA Program from a model by Paul Mohapel (paul.mohapel@shaw.ca)"

Rank each statement as follows:

0 - Never 1 - Rarely 2 - Sometimes 3 - Often 4 - Always

Emotional Awareness

My feelings are clear to me at any given moment	
Emotions play an important part in my life	
My moods impact the people around me	
I find it easy to put words to my feelings	
My moods are easily affected by external events	
I can easily sense when I'm going to be angry	
I readily tell others my true feelings	
I find it easy to describe my feelings	
Even when I'm upset, I'm aware of what's happening to me	
I am able to stand apart from my thoughts and feelings and examine them	

Emotional Awareness Total:

Rank each statement as follows:

0 - Never 1 - Rarely 2 - Sometimes 3 - Often 4 - Always

Emotional Management

I accept responsibility for my reactions	
I find it easy to make goals and stick with them	
I am an emotionally balanced person	
I am a very patient person	
I can accept critical comments from others without becoming angry	
I maintain my composure, even during stressful times	
If an issue does not affect me directly, I don't let it bother me	
I can restrain myself when I feel anger towards someone	
I control urges to overindulge in things that could damage my well being	
I direct my energy into creative work or hobbies	

Emotional Management Total:

Rank each statement as follows:

0 - Never 1 - Rarely 2 - Sometimes 3 - Often 4 - Always

Social Emotional Awareness

I consider the impact of my decisions on other people	
I can tell easily if the people around me are becoming annoyed	
I sense it when a person's mood changes	
I am able to be supportive when giving bad news to others	
I am generally able to understand the way other people feel	
My friends can tell me intimate things about themselves	
It genuinely bothers me to see other people suffer	
I usually know when to speak and when to be silent	
I care what happens to other people	
I understand when people's plans change	

Social Emotional Awareness Total:

Rank each statement as follows:

0 - Never 1 - Rarely 2 - Sometimes 3 - Often 4 - Always

Relationship Management

I am able to show affection	
My relationships are a safe place for me	
I find it easy to share my deep feelings with others	
I am good at motivating others	
I am a fairly cheerful person	
It is easy for me to make friends	
People tell me I am sociable and fun	
I like helping people	
Others can depend on me	
I am able to talk someone down if they are very upset	

Relationship Management Total:

My EQ strengths!

Mark your EQ total scores to assess your strengths and areas for improvement.

Emotional Intelligence

Emotional Awareness	0 2 4 6 8 10 12 14 16 18 20 22 24 26 28 30 32 34 36 38 40
Emotional Management	0 2 4 6 8 10 12 14 16 18 20 22 24 26 28 30 32 34 36 38 40
Social Emotional Awareness	0 2 4 6 8 10 12 14 16 18 20 22 24 26 28 30 32 34 36 38 40
Relationship Management	0 2 4 6 8 10 12 14 16 18 20 22 24 26 28 30 32 34 36 38 40

Measure your effectiveness in each domain using this key:

0—24 Area for enrichment: Requires attention and development

25—34 Effective Functioning: consider strengthening

35—40 Enhanced Skills: Use as leverage to develop weaker areas

Using your EQ strength—for your strongest EQ domain, give an example of how you demonstrate your strength in your daily life or work:

_____

_____

_____

_____

_____

_____

Increase your EQ strength—for your weakest EQ domain, give an example of how this affects you AND others in your daily life or work:

_____

_____

_____

_____

_____

_____

Improving your EQ strength—for your strongest EQ domain, what steps can you take to strengthen yourself in this area? How will this benefit you in your daily life or work?

_____

_____

_____

_____

_____

_____

Johari Window—Responsibility for Impact

The Johari window is a technique used to help people better understand their relationship with themselves and others. You will need a flip chart or white board to document results as shown below:

OPEN	BLIND
HIDDEN	UNKNOWN

1. Introduce the Johari Window concept

2. Provide each person with a copy of "Johari Window Descriptors". The person receiving insights will choose 12 adjectives that best describe themselves. The other participants will each choose 8 adjectives that best describe the individual receiving insights.

3. Then have each participant reveal one adjective they feel represents the individual being assessed. Ask the individual if the adjective was on her list. If it is, place it in the OPEN box and if it isn't, place it in the BLIND BOX.

4. Continue around the group one by one until there have been at least 10 OPEN adjectives listed.

5. The individual is then asked to reveal any remaining adjectives that have not yet been identified by participants.

It may be that an individual identified the adjective but the sharing process ended before they shared the adjective. If this happens add it to the OPEN list. If no one has an adjective that the individual reveals then it should be placed in the HIDDEN box.

6. After all the documentation has been completed, some questions to ask the participant can include:

    •   What were the biggest surprises to you regarding the Blind Spots?

    •   Which adjectives may be helpful to you since you now know others perceptions and observations?

    •   What Hidden adjectives would you like to show more often to your team members?

    •   What would be the first step you could take to move in this direction?

Johari Window Descriptors

Able	Giving	Powerful
Accepting	Happy	Private
Adventurous	Helpful	Proud
Aggressive	Humorous	Quiet
Assertive	Idealistic	Reflective
Autocratic	Impulsive	Relaxed
Autonomous	Independent	Reliable
Bold	Influential	Religious
Calm	Ingenious	Responsive
Caring	Innovative	Risk Taker
Cheerful	Inspirational	Searching
Clever	Intelligent	Self Aware
Complex	Introverted	Self Conscious
Compliant	Intuitive	Self Contained
Confident	Kind	Sensible
Courageous	Knowledgeable	Sentimental
Critical	Listener	Shy
Decisive	Logical	Silly
Demanding	Loving	Spiritual
Dependable	Loyal	Spontaneous
Dignified	Mature	Systematic
Diplomatic	Modest	Talkative
Dominating	Motivator	Tenacious
Empathetic	Nervous	Tense
Energetic	Observant	Thorough
Even-tempered	Open	Trustworthy
Extroverted	Organized	Warm
Flexible	Patient	Wise
Friendly	Persuasive	Witty

Articulate the POOP™ to Dispose of it

Goal: Is to dig deeper for clarity and understanding of what is really going on.

Articulating what's going on is a pure form of **genuine curiosity** in service of awakening a hunger for something better.

"Take some time out to visit various departments in your organisation and be a "fly on the wall" as you visit. Your intention is to identify what the "mood" is in the environment. This takes genuine curiosity and consciousness of your own impact as you enter the room/environment. How do the various departments differ from each other? What did you notice? How does this align to the "mood" with the leadership environment? What are you confirming?"

Now it's time to Dispose Of The POOP™!

Qualities of articulating what is going on:

1. Without judgement and/or interpretation

2. Comes from a place of genuine curiosity

3. Speak in the first person e.g. "I"

4. Typically starts with…
   a. what I sense is…
   b. what I see is…
   c. what I hear is…
   d. what I feel is…

5. And followed with powerful questions to gain clarity on what's going on.

EXAMPLES:

- *I'm sensing...frustration right now.*
  > *What are your thoughts?*
  > *What do you see is going on?*
  > *How does this impact you?*
  > *What's not being said?*

- *What I see...is people getting distracted.*
  > *I'm curious what that is about?*
  > *What's behind ### that?*
  > *What's not being said?*

- *I hear you say...that nothing is working.*
  > *What do you mean by that?*
  > *What is leading you to say/believe that?*
  > *How does that impact you?*

- *What I feel is #####...*
  > *Where is that coming from?*
  > *What contributed that?*
  > *What triggered that?*
  > *How does that make you feel?*

Stages To Dispose Of The POOP™

1. Clarify the need.

2. Brainstorm solutions.

3. Agree to the solution.

4. Identify who is taking ownership of the disposal.

5. Identify if cascading communications are required.

6. Set a deadline.

7. Follow-up to ensure successful disposal.

STEP 3

. . . .

ALIGNMENT

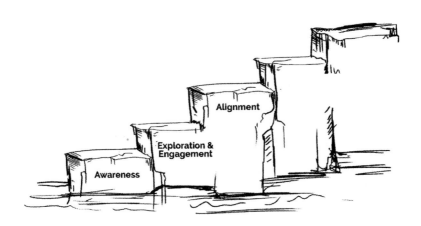

Alignment

Exploration &
Engagement

Awareness

CHAPTER 6

....

Aligning Around the High Dream

After the Exploration and Engagement phase is complete, everyone on the leadership team of the organisation should see themselves as an integral part of moving the organisation forward. As their leader, you've heard everyone's voices, and all have had a chance to share what they're struggling with. You've also taken the time to discover and flush out all the POOP™.

In chapter 2, we introduced Harry, the head of the Saudi Arabian branch of a multi-national transportation company. Harry hired us to help transform his leadership into a team that worked the best that it could be, together. Contrary to what you might expect, when we arrived the branch was actually performing quite well. But Harry's research with their customer base indicated that their organisation was the best of a mediocre bunch. He was understandably concerned that they were not giving their customers enough reasons to stay loyal.

Harry understood that a motivated workforce would provide better value to their customers. He knew that his organisation couldn't properly focus on customers until their leaders were aligned with the company purpose and its high dream and brought out the best in each other. Though some of the leaders got along well, many others lacked trust in one another. A few even showed contempt (a toxic behaviour) for their colleagues.

"Stanley," who had an MBA from a prestigious university, for example, was constantly trying to prove that he was the smartest guy in the room. He made it a point to look down on many of his colleagues and dismiss their contributions. "Janice," on the other hand, felt that her input was overlooked so often that there was no point in expressing her opinion. She withdrew emotionally from the job and sulked quietly during meetings. Neither of these behaviours were benefiting the company to be the best it can be.

In the company at large, the sales, customer service, accounting and fulfilment departments were completely segregated from one another. Not only were they unaware of what the others did all day, they sometimes actively undermined one another's performance. The company was functioning, but the polarity was getting worse. To do nothing was not an option for Harry.

Focusing on the High Dream

There's an old saying that if you don't know where you're going, any road will take you there. Aligning with the high dream is all about knowing exactly where you're going and being fully **committed** to the journey. It's about more than running away from the POOP™; it's about running toward the best.

The high dream for the organisation is the vision for the absolute best the organisation can do and be, and it is the rallying point for alignment. Harry's company described their high dream in great detail and named it "Our Land." When they spoke of Our Land, everyone immediately not only had a clear picture in their heads of what that meant but also felt deeply invested in what it stood for.

Remember, the high dream is not just about what you desire to accomplish, but also whom you are being while you are accomplishing. The values of the organisation, as well as its goals, start to emerge. The **ICE**™ is thick and smooth, meaning that the Infrastructure, Consciousness and Eco-Wisdom™ are strong. This allows both polar bears and penguins to thrive, as the organisations core values connect with the personal values of each team member.

Once you have addressed the POOP™ and the Toxic Waste we discussed in the last chapter, you'll find that it's much easier to generate excitement about becoming a high performing company. Remember, almost everyone wants the opportunity to get better at what they do, just as the overwhelming majority of people do not like doing a job that doesn't make them feel competent and capable. Once you've moved past most people's POOP™, fears, insecurities and misconceptions, most of them will be ready to get to work.

For some, the most important part of the high dream will be strengthening relationships and encouraging cooperation. For others, it will be the establishment of protocols and the precise adherence to best practices. For still others, it will be systematic planning and goal setting. The beautiful part is that, in the high dream, people with each different personality type see their jobs as guarding and nurturing a particular aspect of the organisation's vision. They don't change who they are, but rather gain an understanding for how what they do fits into the big picture. As well, having an appreciation for their co-workers' roles.

In establishing the high dream, there is no judging, no right and wrong, it is what your team believes it can be. It identifies what is possible in your organisation, what is great about working in your organisation and what your customers rave about. It is literally brainstorming and throwing up on the flipchart what it means to you and your team.

We invite you to do an exercise with your leadership team to get them excited about what's possible for you and your organisation. This is at the end of this chapter. Remember, this is truly a brain storming, fun, engaging and creative beginning to the next phase of the process. It is recommended it is done in an off-site, casual and neutral environment.

Alignment is a Choice

The key to effective alignment is the power of being at choice. Not only do we articulate what we want for ourselves and for the organisation, we articulate what we can do to get to what we want. This means we take responsibility for facilitating the change we want to see, and we feel empowered to bring it about. When everyone in your organisation can articulate clearly what the high dream is, they are more easily able to consciously choose to align or not.

Remember that the POOP™—all the pessimism and cynicism we covered in the last chapter—is just as powerful as the high dream; it simply takes everyone to a different place. In some ways the POOP™ can be even more seductive, because it takes less vulnerability to follow. Effective leaders will continually articulate the high dream in a way that resonates with all the different types of people in the organisation. They will demonstrate that they are personally emotionally invested in the on-going transformation of the organisation and in the ultimate outcome of the goals.

When people align with the high dream, they take ownership of it. If job security is important to them, they ask themselves, "How can I contribute to building job security in our organisation?" Furthermore, alignment is both empowering and contagious. Just as people feed off of one another's negativity, they can feed off one another's enthusiasm.

A very useful exercise is to ask employees who rated question #5 (How committed are you to the High Dream?) below an 8, to ask them what it would take to get them to an 8 or above? This must not be confused with how close they believe the company is achieving it. That is a separate matter altogether. Rather than offering accusations or criticisms, this exercise is about articulating what each person needs to completely buy into the high dream.

Of course taking ownership of the high dream involves a certain amount of risk. It's important to emphasise that when the organisation is at its best, risk and even failure are encouraged. Short-term failures are an inevitable side effect of serious attempts at innovation, and so they are accepted as part of growth.

Many people will want to know how their own career advancement fits in with the high dream for the organisation. Where does an individual's high dream for himself or herself coincide with the organisation's vision? Ultimately, when the organisation is at its best, everyone is growing and developing both professionally and personally, so there is room for almost anyone's personal ambitions to be realised.

Of course human nature dictates that toxic behaviours and POOP™ will periodically re-emerge. But the aligned workplace community is empowered to recognise these and deal with them effectively when they come up. Often, simply recognising and naming them is enough to keep them from becoming a systemic problem again. If fear and negativity re-emerge on a large enough scale, however, it may be necessary to go back to the explore and engage stage and reassess the relationship design. Depending on what you find, you may want to refine the relationship further.

Moving from Competition to Collaboration

A car could have four perfectly good tyres, but if they are not properly aligned, they will wear out prematurely. When you take your car for an alignment, the mechanics don't change anything about the tyres themselves; they simply adjust the angles of the wheels to the manufacturer's specifications. This ensures that the vehicle will drive straight and reduces unnecessary friction.

Alignment in your organisation is a similar concept. You are not achieving alignment by making a polar bear into a penguin or vice versa. You are merely adjusting the connection between each person and the organisation itself. Diverse organisations have to stretch further to achieve alignment, but the opportunity for growth is also greater.

Aligned organisations produce synergy: the increased effectiveness that comes from cooperative work. But before we can expect true synergy, we must build empathy. Polar bears can ask themselves what it feels like to be a penguin and vice versa. The same goes for different workplace personality profiles and members of different departments.

Just like in Harry's transportation company, it's very easy for different departments to undermine one another rather than working cooperatively. In a software company, for example, programmers may resent the sales department for making promises to customers that are challenging or impossible for the programmers to keep. The sales department may resent the programmers for not understanding the customers' needs. To add fuel to the fire, most programmers will probably have a different workplace style and possibly even a different cultural background from the sales staff.

But what happens when sales staff and programmers work intentionally to develop empathy for one another? Instead of being unconsciously competent at a job that comes naturally to them, they become aware of how incredibly challenging the other job is. They become "consciously incompetent." In the process, they develop an appreciation for what the people in the other department do. When the sales staff sees the thousands of lines of code that go into the delivering the product to the customer—and realises that one misplaced 0 or 1 can throw everything off—they develop genuine admiration for the programmers. And likewise, the programmers experience gratitude when they learn how many phone calls, meetings and emails are involved with bringing the client to sign on the dotted line, without which no one, including the programmers, will get paid.

When this kind of empathy and appreciation becomes the norm, polar bears and penguins can move from living competitively in the organisation to living in harmony. Before the sales team makes a promise, they'll consider what kind of burden it might place on the programmers. Before the programmers leave at the end of their work week, they'll go the extra mile to make sure the sales team can keep its promise.

When the company is living the high dream, everyone becomes aware of their strengths and weaknesses while also discovering untapped talent in themselves and one another. One of the benefits of exploring what goes on in other departments is learning about other skills or potential that isn't being completely harnessed by the organisation. This leads to greater collaboration and minimises the tendency of some to be protective of their own "territory." People begin to think beyond what is required of them on paper to consider what others need from them in order to do their jobs well.

When we learn to appreciate the contribution of others and empathise with their challenges, the cooperative energy flourishes. When all employees in the organisation feel that their co-workers—even in other departments, from different cultural backgrounds, or of different personality profiles—appreciate their challenges, struggles and frustrations, they are much better equipped to align with and work toward that high dream together.

Exploring the triumphs and struggles of other "species" also allows people to celebrate every achievement of the organisation, rather than just their personal ones. This new perspective also opens minds and sparks greater curiosity, innovation, and creativity.

Brainstorming the High Dream

Purpose: This is an exercise to explore what is possible for the organisation and getting people excited about it.

Process: On a flip chart, carved in sand, covered in post-it notes capture the brainstorming ideas elicited from the below questions and take a photo before the tide comes in!

If your organisation were as good as it could get...

1. What would it achieve?

2. What behaviours would be seen to get those achievements?

3. What is great about working here?

4. What is the environment like in this "high dream" place?

5. How do you behave in the "high dream" place?

6. What are your customers raving about?

List EVERYTHING on the flipchart without judgement.

Examples of High Dream characteristics—do you need to import any onto your list?:

- Alignment
- On purpose
- Clear communication
- Proactive
- Clear expectations
- Recognition & appreciation
- Commitment
- Quality work
- Growth orientated
- Promotion
- Involvement
- Connected to each other
- Celebration
- Encouragement
- Creative
- See & know their path
- Playing to their own unique strengths
- Caring
- Strong relationships
- Authentic
- Transparent
- Clear boundaries
- Permission to fail
- Fun & play

- Humour
- Discretionary effort
- I'm heard & seen
- Empowerment
- Positive intent
- Training (I'm invested in)
- Right person right job
- Career progression
- Market leader
- Increased market share
- Employee benefits
- Bonuses
- Integrity & respect
- Reputation
- Innovation
- Role models
- Job security
- High confidence
- Teamwork
- Productiveness
- Loyalty
- Hope
- Patience
- Self discipline
- Efficiencies

- Belonging
- Harmony
- Profitability
- Regular performance feedback
- Fast to market
- Organisation expands
- Unity
- Healthy
- Pride
- Passion
- Best practices
- Ethical
- Responsibility

- Openness
- Living brand values
- Friendly
- My opinion matters
- Open minded
- Receptive
- Cheerful
- Increase of right customers
- Consideration
- Repeat business increases
- Follow-up/through
- Promises are kept
- Coaching

Lesson: Questions to now ask everyone:

1. On a scale of 1-10 (10 being totally connected to the high dream) where are you on the continuum today?
2. What are your insights?
3. What are you learning about yourself, the team and your organisation?
4. What are you choosing?
5. On a scale of 1-10 how committed are you to the High Dream?

Exercise—To Align

At your next leadership team meeting, create an environment where each functional head can share safely their challenges, struggles and frustrations of daily life in that function/department. This requires people to be fully transparent, open and tolerant where everyone honours and appreciates the current reality without judgement or

POOP™ (Preconceived Ideas, Obstacles, Obsessions and Prejudices). Once shared the group is then asked the following questions:

1. What's the most important thing you just heard?
2. What are the challenges and pressures?
3. How does this department/role need help and support?
4. What is needed to be fully aligned?
5. How do we hold each other accountable to the needs?

Now that Harry's organisation has aligned, he has found that his employees have a great deal more trust in one another. When people have differences of opinion, they assume that others are trying to help them not undermine them. They are collaborating at a much higher level and their professional camaraderie is much richer than ever before.

Stanley no longer feels the need to be the smartest guy in the room. He has a new respect and appreciation for his fellow leaders, and he's much more pleasant to be around. He has also become much better at his job, because he understands how it fits into the bigger picture, knows what he doesn't know, and stays in his lane. Jane has come out of her shell and contributes energetically (in her own quiet way) to the planning and direction of the organisation.

Although only the leaders went through the workshop that was conducted, the skills they learned enabled them to relate to and communicate with the rest of the employees much more effectively. They are more transparent, they listen better and they understand their strengths and weaknesses much better than before. And within just a few weeks of the workshop, they were able to accelerate some of the projects and initiatives that had been stalling for months.

Ultimately, aligning with the high dream involves an individual commitment to transparency, openness and tolerance. It also requires a group commitment to honouring and appreciating one another's contributions. As each of us strives to be the best we can be, we build something so much greater together.

STEP 4

. . . .

COMMITMENT

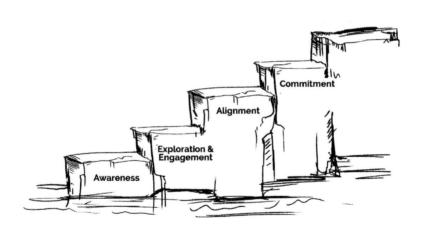

CHAPTER 7

....

Define your Culture

Rome wasn't built in a day. It takes time and deliberate, consistent effort to build a culture in your organisation that affirms and harnesses the power of a diverse group of employees. The good news is that this task really can be accomplished in a finite period of time, usually eighteen months to a couple of years. Best of all, the positive effects—if properly nurtured—can last decades.

So, even if you have skipped to this part of the book—just to get a feel for the work we do—you absolutely cannot skip the phases we've outlined in the previous chapters to achieve that kind of unity. The harmonious ownership of both purpose and values that truly healthy organisations enjoy, is the destination of a very intentional journey. There are proven strategies to get there, but there are no short cuts.

Just as with anything else in life, smaller changes implemented consistently over time are far more powerful in the long run than dramatic changes enacted quickly. The same action—such as rewriting the company's mission statement and values—has a completely different impact when it is enacted suddenly with little explanation compared to when it is the culmination of a collective process of rethinking and rebuilding the organisation. The first will likely be abandoned and forgotten within a few months; the second—when the leadership team is committed to live it out—is much more likely to transform the organisation in a lasting way.

To lead a diverse organisation effectively requires patience, tenacity and a heart level commitment to the principles we've outlined in the previous chapters. It takes genuine concern for the people you lead and work with. But when those qualities are authentically present, they are shockingly contagious. They begin to spread organically to the rest of the organisation even beyond the intentional efforts of the leadership.

Think about a large sporting event such as a football match (or soccer, as Americans like to say!). No one has to tell the crowd to cheer when their team scores; they do so automatically out of both the passion they feel for their team, and the cultural expectations of the crowd around them. Someone who is quiet and shy may cheer almost as loudly as someone who is naturally boisterous. Race, education level and professional expertise rarely interfere with the unity of purpose and passion that fans feel when they are cheering for the same team.

By contrast, most art museums often evoke quite the opposite response from their visitors. Even the chatty types usually quiet down before the great masterpieces displayed in each room. Such places produce a contemplative mood in all who enter. And although it's fair to say that a museum may attract a slightly different crowd from a football match, the environment of each is still the primary influencer on the behaviour of the people involved.

In the same way, you can build a work culture that is so powerful that it draws all your employees into the right behaviours and discourages them from the behaviours that don't serve. The environment of your company can be so positive that everyone wants to be a part of it. And before long, the behaviours you are looking for become second nature.

Sustainable Accountability

Because all human beings are imperfect, we need accountability in order to live our best lives. Left to our own devices, we may deviate from all that we can be. The organisational culture you worked so hard to build is made up of imperfect individuals who are no exception to this rule; they too need accountability to thrive. Our default behaviours are not necessarily harmonious, so we have to help one another along to ensure we don't slip back into our old ways.

But there are different kinds of accountability. Some organisations—like the military for example—enforce strict, top-down accountability so that they can be prepared for life and death situations. Because of this, members sign away certain rights as a condition of joining. Some people may even choose this style of accountability when they join certain weight loss or exercise programs, for example, because they worry that they won't follow through with their commitment without the threat of embarrassment.

That kind of accountability, however, is not sustainable over the long term for normal situations. People cannot thrive in an environment where their primary motivation for doing the right thing or abiding by the rules is the threat of punishment or humiliation. They will begin to resent the source of the threats, which will ultimately undermine their engagement at work. So how can we hold each other accountable in a way that continues to nurture respectful, trusting relationships?

The best form of accountability is conspicuously living out the values of the organisation, starting with the leadership team itself. It is this on-going, consistent behaviour from leadership that creates and reinforces the cultural norms of the organisation. From there, it is natural to affirm others who are doing the same, and, when necessary, correct or adjust those who fail to do so. The key to this feedback being meaningful is the correlation of their behaviour rightly or wrongly, to the core values.

Pretend for a moment that the cultural norm you wanted to establish and enforce was for everyone to wear black to work every Monday. You would start by getting a commitment from the leadership to wear black every Monday; then you would explain the behaviour to everyone by sending out a memorandum, and perhaps even meeting with them in person. After that, you would begin to openly affirm people who showed up wearing black on Mondays, and then, after the norm was well established, you might begin speaking privately with those who were not wearing black on Mondays.

Now of course wearing a certain colour to work is a completely arbitrary idea that no company would choose to implement without a good reason. But the principles for implementation hold true for almost any behaviour you would like to see. Suppose one of your values is respect for everyone's time. You might begin by securing a commitment from the entire leadership team to be on time to work and to each scheduled meeting. Then you would explain the value to everyone in the organisation. You would then begin affirming people who show up early or on time, and, once the habits were well established among the leadership, you could begin speaking privately with those who still seem to struggle with the behaviour. (It's important also to praise and affirm effort, even if a person is still struggling to make the behaviour a habit.)

But it is easy to see how no value will take hold unless the leadership team is committed to lead by example. This doesn't mean they all have to be perfect, but it means that when they violate the behaviour they should offer an unconditional apology that acknowledges the value that has been violated. When leaders take the values seriously, almost everyone else will follow suit with no argument. When they don't, it is as if they are scolding others for not wearing black while they themselves are sporting bright pink!

Core Values

The kind of people we hire and retain also defines and affirms what we value. Hiring for culture is vital, because we really cannot compromise the way we treat each other each day, regardless of how otherwise qualified a candidate may be. If we sacrifice our values for knowledge and skill, the ICE™ will break apart.

It is also important that the leadership team periodically evaluate everyone in the company to determine individuals' alignment to the core values. Are the most productive employees actively living out the value in question? Are the least productive employees ignoring or undermining it? If the answer to either of these questions is "yes", it may be time to rethink the value itself or the people!

For example, we worked with an organisation that insisted on a particular value of "care". But only about 25 per cent of the leadership was caring to those within the organisation. The other 75 per cent were not caring to anyone, including each other. Still, they insisted this was one of their core values, and so we helped them with the process of forcing it into their culture.

As you might expect, the value never took hold, because the leadership did not live it out. They did hire people who possessed this value, but then those people began to leave, because they saw that the value was not an authentic part of the organisation.

Finally, the leadership was able to see that their true core values did not quite match this particular aspirational value. They realised that "care" was actually a brand promise to their customers, not an internal value shaping how they treated one another. So they removed it from their core values, and kept it as a brand promise for their customer service.

Culture will Eat Strategy for Breakfast

As Peter Drucker says "Culture, will eat strategy for breakfast". In other words, you can have the best laid out plan and strategy, pay fortunes for it, but if your culture is toxic, full of POOP™ and/or is not honouring the core values, it will not be high performing.

Now let's explore what the core values are for your organisation. Harvard's Business Review article by Patrick Lencioni entitled "Make Your Values Mean Something" defines core values as: "Deeply ingrained principles that guide all of a company's actions; they serve as its cultural cornerstones. They can never be compromised, either for convenience or short term economic gain. They are a source of company's distinctiveness and must be maintained at all costs."

He also says, "If you're not willing to accept the pain real values incur, don't bother going to the trouble of formulating values!"

Real values are the DNA of your organisation and represent the organisation's being. There may be times when it is commercially attractive to deviate from the core values for an element of short term material gain or win, but it goes against the values... the pain comes when you honour your values because this is "who" you are as an organisation and nothing can compromise that.

One of the first things many leaders do is hand off the development of values to the HR department or an external agency, which uses the initiative as an excuse for a feel good effort. That is precisely the wrong approach. Firstly, involving all employees in the development of values integrates suggestions from employees who may not belong in the company in the first place. Secondly, it leads employees to believe that all input is equally valuable. The best values development is driven by a small team that include the CEO, any founders and other key stake holders including the senior leadership team. Values are a set of fundamental, strategic sound behaviours that drive business results for your organisation.

To develop, validate or refine your organisation's core values, facilitate the exercise at the end of this chapter with the leadership team. As a gentle reminder, this is NOT a task to be delegated!

Now that your core values are nailed down, if they are really going to take hold in your organisation they need to be integrated into every employee related process including: hiring, performance managing, promotions and rewards and even dismissal. We will discuss more of this in the final chapters.

Moving Forward

Why do we all come to work every day, beyond the pay cheque? Ultimately, the behaviours we value are rooted in the purpose and high dream for the organisation. When people truly buy-in and see how their roles contribute to that higher purpose, they will be motivated to do a great job.

Susan worked with a restaurant recently to help them clarify their core purpose, which was to "wow customers with a culinary and hospitality experience by feeding all five senses". Every employee bought into this purpose and was on the same page. They all understood how their jobs—whether they were in the kitchen or on the wait staff—contributed to this overall dream. The management led by example and employees were regularly affirmed when they did things well.

What the restaurant leadership began to see is that the behaviours (values) that were aligned to the core purpose became second nature. Just as you don't have to remind yourself every day to brush your teeth or tie your shoes, their employees didn't need to be told to smile at customers or prepare food to the expected standard. The leadership team hired, trained, performance managed, recognised and rewarded people who lived and breathed the core purpose and values every day because they knew what contributions their work had on the business outcomes. The leaders within the organisation won the hearts and minds of the people that worked for them, as they too practiced what they preached. Because of this they achieved record growth.

Now take a few minutes to think of your organisation's reason for being. As Harry Beckwith once said "People don't lead, purposes do".

Consider these questions: What is you organisation's core purpose (mission statement)?—In other words, when your employees are on their way to work every day, what do you want them to be saying is their purpose? For example, we know Disney employees come to work to make people happy. Google's employees come to work every day to organise the world's information and make it universally accessible and useful and Walmart employees help people save money so they can live better.

The commonality between these three is what makes up a good purpose statement. Every employee can see their role and responsibilities within it. As a leadership team, start answering the following questions to identify what your organisational purpose is:

1. What do we do?

2. What makes us different?

3. For whom do we do it?

4. Why does our organisation's existence matter?

5. What is our most important reason for being here? Why?

6. What would be lost if this organisation ceased to exist?

7. Why are we important to the people we serve?

8. Why would anyone dedicate their precious time, energy, and passion to our company? (Note: the answer is not money.)

Defining your core purpose is all about clarity, authenticity, and alignment. This means that you do not have to sound "sexy." This is not something that has to sound impressive on a billboard. It does, however, have to feel meaningful. You'll know when you finally identify your core purpose because it will be accompanied by a strong sense of conviction. The team will feel a deep "yes!" when it is uncovered.

Other features of an effective core purpose are:

✓ Short and sweet (like powerful questions, are 7 words or less)

✓ Concentrates on the present

✓ It evokes passion

✓ Everyone can see themselves playing a part

✓ Its beyond just making money

✓ Anchors employees daily activities

✓ It identifies the responsibilities the organisation has towards its clients.

The work culture, as embraced and lived out by each leader and employee, is organic. It will be both reaffirmed and refined over time. As the needs of the organisation change, there may be corresponding changes in the culture. This means that we don't need to feel pressured to get it perfect right away.

BIG HAIRY AUDACIOUS GOAL (BHAG)

What is a BHAG? A Big Hairy Audacious Goal is a statement of Strategic Intention—the specific result the organisation will achieve in 10-30 years time. It is the inspiring "Mount Everest" they will climb. It is one of the components of the company's high dream, as per the Jim Collins and Gerry Porras book, "Built to Last".

Key attributes of a good BHAG are:

✓ Inspiring—motivates everyone in the organisation

✓ Possible—not easy, but it could be achieved if the whole organisation operated at the top of their game.

✓ The BHAG must be set with a realistic understanding of what the organisation can achieve.

✓ Fits with organisation's purpose and values

✓ Consistent—the BHAG will have no credibility if the business changes it every few years.

✓ A BHAG that is big enough to inspire and will take a decade of extraordinary effort to deliver.

Why is it useful? It is a very powerful way to communicate a clear direction and level of ambition that aligns the whole organisation. The leadership team must be committed to the BHAG, or it will not only have no power, it will reduce credibility.

Just like the purpose statement, don't force it artificially—when it comes it will immediately feel right.

An example from Starbucks is to overtake Coke as the world's leading brand. It is a good example of alignment with company purpose and values. The Starbucks BHAG is about world-class brand-building—at the heart of their purpose and values, is not number of stores or revenue targets. And it will take the company performing at their best for 20 years to reach.

An example from Sony in the 1960's and 70's is to change the image of "Made in Japan" from poor quality to high quality.

A non-profit example is John F Kennedy's 1961 speech to Congress: "I believe that this nation should commit itself to achieving the goal, before this decade is out, of landing a man on the moon and returning him safely to the earth…We choose to go to the moon in this decade and do the other things. Not because they are easy, but because they are hard."

Now it's time to look at "who" you have in your team to make all of this happen.

Articulating Values

Purpose: Organisational values are a company's ethical and moral compass and decision-making foundation. They are the ideals and ethics that management holds dear. They drive decision-making in that they are constantly referred to in the decision-making process. That is, when you are in a tough spot, the answer needs, first and foremost, to be consistent with the organisation's values. They are generally for both internal and external consumption. They tell those in the company how things are done and those outside the company why they want to be associated with this organisation. Organisational values are best when they are few in number (between 3-7) but high in meaning and lived daily.

Process:

1. Individually identify 3-5 top performers in your organisation today who are considered role models for others to emulate— Who are they?

2. Of these people—List all the behaviours that lead you to believe they are top performers.

3. Share as a group the behaviours associated with top performers and list on a flipchart

4. Relook at your High Dream, and identify behaviours that truly represent who you are as an organisation… Take these into this exercise.

5. Organise or group all identified behaviours into similar or related words. For example, integrity, truth, honesty, honour, openness, respect

6. As a group discuss one by one if it is believed to be core to your business. It must be of critical importance and essential for the business.

7. As a group, compare how you as a management team role model these behaviours to see if they are really "CORE" to your organisation's culture.

8. Write your names down on the left hand side of the page and the values on the top from left to right. Place a check mark next to the values that each individual on your leadership team does most of the time. Those values that have a majority check mark beside them are CORE to your organisation.

9. Once identified, now create a statement or paragraph that represents the value and provides a definition of what that really means.

10. As a final check, take an underperformer in your organisation and see how many core values he/she does most of the time. Likely you will find that he/she does not live out the core values of the company on a daily basis

Learnings

The following are typical ideas of how core values should appear and be reinforced within your organisation. Examine the list and place a check in the boxes that you need to begin doing or to improve upon as a management team

☐ Recruitment selection criteria

☐ Orientation/Induction

☐ Role of training/training programs

☐ Performance Evaluations/appraisal forms

☐ Team rewards

☐ Individual rewards

- ☐ Strategy decisions

- ☐ Resource allocation

- ☐ Stakeholder relationships

- ☐ New customers and suppliers

- ☐ Policies and procedures

- ☐ Organisational and job design

- ☐ Managing change

- ☐ Operational tasks of quality and service

Where else should they appear and be reinforced within your organisation? How will you communicate and hold people accountable to the values?

CHAPTER 8

....

Embracing Diversity

The high dream, purpose and values belong to everyone in the company, not just the CEO. Within the world of that high dream, it is essential that everyone feels they are free to advance as far as their Desire, Ability and Commitment will carry them. The connection phase rises and falls on the leadership's demonstration of their own connection to the high dream and the behaviours that underpin it.

By now, you have a lot of good ideas about how to begin to build bridges between polar bears and penguins. But people don't differ only by roles and responsibilities, culture or ethnicity. Every human being is different from every other. We all have our own distinct fingerprints, signatures and DNA profiles. In addition to being an original combination of genetic material, every person on earth has had a unique combination of experiences and relationships. So even in a culturally homogenous organisation, there is a tremendous diversity of personalities and preferences.

For true commitment, healthy relationships are required at all levels. In other words we need to be able to manage relationships effectively in a non-judgemental, non-repercussions, non-reprisal kind of way. Each leader needs to take responsibility for their impact and be genuinely curious about the impact others have on them.

One of the most useful ways to think about these individual differences is by understanding the patterns of behaviour that we exhibit when confronted with typical situations. As individuals, how do we deal with problems and challenges? With people and contacts? With preferred pace and level of consistency? And, with procedures and constraints?

Contrary to popular belief, a high performing culture is not one that is always conflict-free. It's really easy to avoid conflict by surrounding yourself with people who share your temperament and preferences, or who just accept without being fully committed, but that is not necessarily the best way to build a high performing organisation. Most organisations need people with a variety of gifts and abilities, and many times those come packaged in different personalities and dispositions. Transformational leaders are not threatened by those with different Desires, Abilities and Commitment, and work to integrate everyone's strengths for the betterment of the organisation and achieving the high dream.

We worked with the CEO of a bank where nearly everyone he

employed loved to debate ideas, strategies and methods, much like himself. In theory, this was a wonderful way for him to access everyone's voice and for the bank to benefit from the wisdom and experience of each employee. However, we found he actually felt threatened by this diversity and built walls instead of bridges. In hindsight the CEO had the Ability to embrace diversity, but he did not have the Desire or Commitment. All of the work in the previous phases (Awareness, Exploration and Engagement, Alignment and Connection) was jeopardised. One of the big learnings in this experience for the CEO was that he needed to be Fully Committed to hearing all the voices within the Eco-system even when things got a little turbulent. He needed to be Fully Present With What Is, Take Responsibility for his Impact and believe the Answers were Within to navigate the storm. A friendly reminder to the guiding principles for a high-performing culture.

The second big learning for the CEO was that he was expecting members on his team to adapt to a behaviour that went against their natural tendencies. Adaptability is important for situations when they arise; however, adaptability 100% of the time against your natural tendencies leads to burnout and breakdown of commitment.

Needless to say the storm developed further and created plenty of POOP™ and Toxic Behaviours—killing the hunger for something better within the team.

Nearly a century ago, Dr. William Moulton Marston introduced the concept of the DISC personality profile, focusing on behaviour tendencies that were directly observable. Unlike many other psychological theories rooted in abstractions, DISC was developed for a very practical reason: to help people manage their relationships more effectively and embrace diversity.

Effective leaders recognise that various personality styles are expressed differently in different environments. For the remainder of this chapter we'll discuss the four components of the DISC personality profile to help you gain a better understanding of yourself and others on your team.

The classic DISC profile is a needs-motivated profile which measures energy put into how you deal with problems and challenges, how you deal with people and contacts, how you deal with pace and consistency and procedures and constraints. It measures people's emotions, needs and fears.

DISC is **NOT** a measure of intelligence, skills, education or experience or an indicator of values. DISC is a combination of nature (inherent) and nurture (learnt).

We have been brought up to interact with others by the "golden rule", which is treating others the way you would like to be treated. While that is a great rule to live by much of the time, it doesn't always work with communication. Instead, we ask you to consider Dr. Tony Alessandra's Platinum Rule®—Treat others the way THEY want to be treated to communicate as effectively as possible. To be a high performing culture/team where a diverse group of employees can thrive in any weather condition, we must seek to understand them. DISC is a way to help us do that.

The DISC model describes four different styles: Dominance (D), Influence (I), Steadiness (S) and Conscientiousness (C), All of us possess all four components in some measure, but usually one or two tend to govern the way we prefer to work. No style is right or wrong, but people with each style tend to have certain strengths, needs and weaknesses. By learning more about each, we learn more about ourselves, our co-workers and those who makes up our organisation

Dominance (D)—Polar Bear

Dominance is how people address problems and challenges. The typical D tends to be direct and guarded much like a Polar Bear. D's often prefer to work alone and they love being in charge. They are often found among the leadership of an organisation, but simply possessing a Dominant personality style does not make one an effective leader. D's are often competitive and can seem a bit pushy at times, and they definitely prefer to communicate directly, instead of negotiating or beating around the bush.

D's are great at taking charge, and they are willing to take risks that would frighten others. They are tough and adaptable, but they often struggle to be patient and sensitive to other people's feelings. They will get things done, but may leave a lot of collateral damage in their wake if they are not self-aware. They do not naturally think about details, so they are famous for offering a vision without the practical steps to achieve it. They are motivated by setting goals and the sense of achievement that comes from reaching them.

Questions to ask yourself:

1. What kind of person comes to mind?

2. How do they walk?

3. How do they talk?

4. What does their workspace look like?

5. What value do they bring to a team?

Influence (I)—Arctic Hare

Influence is how people handle situations involving people and contacts. I's tend to be direct and open, are personable, fun-loving, and love being around others much like the Arctic Hare. They value relationships deeply and don't want to hurt anybody. They can be emotionally sensitive and generally desire popularity. I's can be very charming and persuasive, naturally winning people over to their point of view.

I's are terrific at connecting with others, but they may struggle with assignments that require thoroughness, focus and follow through. They are motivated by social recognition and verbal affirmation, but they are vulnerable to having their feelings hurt. Their focus on people may also hinder their attention to the details of a task.

How I's express themselves is very much shaped by what their cultural norms are for socialising because of their desire to be liked and be popular.

Questions to ask yourself:

1. What kind of person comes to mind?
2. How do they walk?
3. How do they talk?
4. What does their workspace look like?
5. What value do they bring to a team?

Steadiness (S)—Penguin

Steadiness is how people demonstrate pace and consistency. S's tends to be indirect and open. The S style is open to others, but the true emotion of the style is concealed. It appears open but it's not really open at all. S's thrive on cooperation and appreciation, much like that of Penguins in their colonies as they huddle together to conserve heat in order to be adaptable to the Antarctic winter conditions. S's can seem predictable, deliberate and even a little boring, and they often struggle with overcommitting themselves because they have a hard time saying no. They typically have the hardest time adjusting to change in the organisation. Although they don't tend to be as socially outgoing as the I's, they do value social acceptance. S's also struggle to multitask and may be uncomfortable with direct confrontation.

Questions to ask yourself:

1. What kind of person comes to mind?

2. How do they walk?

3. How do they talk?

4. What does their workspace look like?

5. What value do they bring to a team?

Conscientiousness (C)—Leopard Seal

Conscientiousness is how people react to procedure and constraints in the workplace. C's tend be indirect and guarded and often found to be  alone much like that of a Leopard Seal. They are careful, cautious, systematic, accurate and tactful. They prioritise themselves to ensure accuracy, maintain stability and challenge assumptions. They have a deep burning desire to gain knowledge, show their expertise and quality work. They may be limited by being over critical, over analysing and isolating themselves and can show signs of aggression when being criticised or pointed out as being wrong.

C's are all about the rules and following them in everything. They are detail-oriented and risk-averse. Careful and calculating in almost everything they do, they are great at getting things done, but they may struggle to give up control in a situation where they have to work with others. They can be shy and may not like to join in with all the social events the I's arrange. They may also find it challenging to make a decision on their feet, without having the time to weigh all the options carefully.

Questions to ask yourself:

1. What kind of person comes to mind?

2. How do they walk?

3. How do they talk?

4. What does their workspace look like?

5. What value do they bring to a team?

Each behavioural style brings unique abilities and no one style is better than any other. Most of us are a blend of styles, so it is important to identify the most likely style based on observable behaviours to help us communicate more effectively with one another.

Identifying the Four Styles

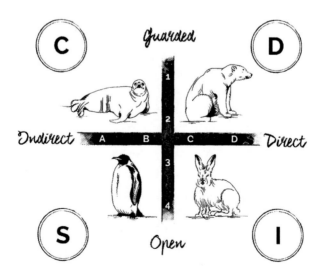

There are two questions you can ask yourself to identify what you and others on your team may be:

1. Are you more direct or indirect?
   a. Using the scale of A-D, choose a letter based on your directness or indirectness.
2. Are you more guarded or open?
   a. Using the scale of 1-4, choose a number based on if you are more guarded or open.

Depending on the number and letter you chose, are you a D, I, S or C? In addition to having differing focuses, tendencies and observable characteristics, each style also has a different pace and priority. These differences can be easily overlooked and can lead to challenges. D & I are faster paced, S & C are slower paced. D & C are task oriented, I & S are people focused.

Pace & Priority

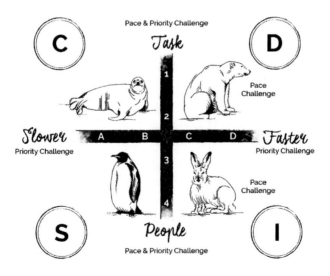

Please ask yourself the following questions:

1. What are the challenges that come from having different paces in your organisation?

2. What challenges come from having different priorities? (i.e. task vs. people)

	D	**I**	**S**	**C**
DISC Focus	**Problems /Tasks**	**People**	**Pace (or Environment)**	**Procedures**
Needs	Challenges to solve, Authority	Social relationships, Friendly environ-ment	Systems, Teams, Stable environ-ment	Rules to follow, Data to analyse
Observable	Decisive, risk-taker	Optimistic, trust others	Patience, stabiliser	Cautious, careful decision
Fears	Being taken advantage of/lack of control	Being left out, loss of social approval	Sudden change/loss of stability and security	Being criticised/ loss of accuracy and quality

Some famous D people include Donald Trump and Martha Stewart. Some famous I people include Jim Carrey, Oprah Winfrey and Ellen Degeneres. Some famous S people include Mother Theresa, Princess Diana and Tom Hanks. Some famous C people include Bill Gates, Warren Buffett and Einstein.

DISC examines our observable behaviours that are driven by our needs and fears.

The above table shows:

- A reminder of the DISC focus of each style
- The needs of each style
- The observable behaviours of each style
- The fears of each style

DISC and Personal Growth

You will find all four of the DISC styles in your organisation and in different parts of yourself. Sometimes you may feel that your style varies by situation or setting. Someone might be a D at work but more of an I at home, for example. The point of utilising these kinds of tools is that awareness of these differences empowers you as a leader to understand yourself and your people better. The goal in becoming educated about the styles is not to make excuses for yourself by saying, "Oh, I'm a D. That's just how I react to these things." Instead, growing leaders will use their knowledge and understanding of the styles to consider their own strengths and weaknesses and to better relate to their co-workers and direct reports and take responsibility for their impact.

Leaders are found among all four-personality types, although each leadership style will be slightly different. Effective leaders will be distinguished by their ability to relate to and communicate well with all four types, regardless of their own personal style. They are aware of their own tendencies and how they might potentially offend or hurt those with different personalities. In other words taking responsibility for their impact.

Emotions

Each DISC style also expresses specific emotions. The D's express anger and impatience. I's express optimism and trust. S's express patience and non-expressiveness (hence why some people find them boring!). C's express fears and concerns.

It is important to be aware of others' challenges and how we can support and be more patient with others' difficulties.

Adaptability

Adaptability is based on two elements; flexibility and aptitude. Flexibility is the willingness and aptitude is your capability to adjust the approach based upon the particular need of the situation or relationship at a particular time. Adaptability does not mean an imitation of the other person's style; it does mean adjusting your openness, directness, pace and priority in the direction of the other persons preference, while maintaining your own identity. Being more adaptable enables more engagement with difficult (those people that are the opposite of you) people and helps to avoid or manage tense situations.

To be more adaptable to other styles, this is what each style needs to be willing to do occasionally:

D's	I's	S's	C's
Show patience Display sensitivity Get into the details Allow deliberation	Follow through completely Research all the facts Speak directly and candidly Stay focus for long periods	Quickly adapt to change or unclear expectations Multitask Promote themselves Confront others	Let go of and delegate tasks Compromise for the good of the team Join in social events and celebrations Make quick decisions

Highly adaptable people determine what types of behaviour are most appropriate in specific situations. When identifying another's style, are they direct or indirect in their communications? Are they guarded or open in their communications? Can you determine the styles on your team by answering these two questions?

By making the choice to be aware and adapt, leaders can work on the best ways to strengthen communication with each other.

Tip for communicating with different styles:

D	I	S	C
Be clear, specific, brief and organised with an agenda	Give them a spot in the limelight	Give them the opportunity to contribute	Be prompt, prepared and precise
Stick to business. Don't force a "personal" relationship	Create an atmosphere of excitement, fun and variety	Be patient. Respond to their questions and concerns	Allow them time to think; be comfortable with silence

Activity—Adapting to DISC Styles

Take a few minutes to explore each of the following questions:

1. My behavioural style is?

2. One person I currently have a professional relationship with is?

3. Based on my observation, this person's behavioural style is?

4. Some sources of stress in this relationship are?

5. I'd like to see my relationship improve in these specific ways?

6. What immediate adjustments to my style will demonstrate adaptability?

7. What strategies will I pursue to strengthen this relationship?

Adapting our style is not always easy; it takes time, practice and patience. For a full DISC profile report for you and your team please visit **www.pbpbooks.com**.

After they take the assessment ask the following questions in a relaxed team environment . We encourage you to take this as a team building opportunity outside of the workplace environment:

Allow the team to one-by-one respond to the below questions:

1. When I'm working on a project or plan I prefer...

2. I am motivated when...

3. When working in a team environment I...

4. When I am emotionally charged / or someone on my team gets emotionally charged I...

5. I get frustrated most when...

6. What I most appreciate from others on my team is...

7. When problem solving I need most...

STEP 5

. . . .

ACCULTURATE

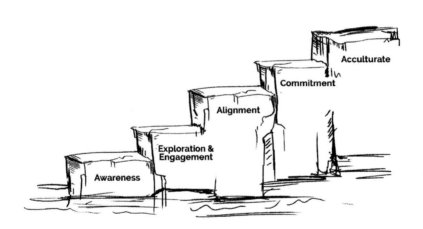

CHAPTER 9

. . . .

Leveraging the Eco-Wisdom™

"Gerald", seemed like a born leader. He had tons of ideas, an assertive personality, and loved to be in charge—the typical behavioural style of a D. He had no problem coming up with a plan and delegating tasks to others. His energy and enthusiasm caught the attention of his superiors, who soon promoted him to management, to his understandable delight.

Gerald attacked his new role with zeal, creating three new initiatives in his first month. What his supervisors soon learned, however, is that his enthusiasm and seemingly natural leadership personality did not equate to skill. His ideas were poorly researched and, while he was generally well liked, he was not deeply respected by his new direct reports. Soon Gerald became discouraged, and the department he was supposed to help lead began to struggle.

What should you consider when you are recruiting, promoting and performance-managing people? Remember, effective leaders are found among all behavioural types; they may just go about leading others in different ways. D's and D/I's may seem like they would be natural leaders—and many are—but someone can have a very strong D personality like Gerald and still be ineffective. Gerald had not yet mastered his ability to be adaptable to the needs of others around him in order for him to capitalise and leverage relationships and talents to the fullest. Had he tapped into a team member who was a C to help him pay attention to detail, or adapted his own style to embrace more C, the outcome would have been very different.

Once your team is beginning to align with the high dream, purpose and values, you can begin to truly leverage the "Eco-Wisdom™" of your organisation. This is where you start to see significant payout on the investment you have put in during the earlier stages. For diverse organisations, this is the stage where what might have been your greatest weakness becomes your greatest strength.

When you are in the habit of engaging both the hearts and minds of your employees, you encourage everyone to not only be on task but to be "on purpose" every day. As the high dream begins to take shape, you will probably see a mixture of reactions: some will instantly feel motivated, anticipating all the exciting developments on the horizon—a typical I, Arctic Hare. Others will feel anxious and apprehensive, not sure of what to expect—a typical C, Leopard Seal. Other will just want to get going and get on with getting the job done—a typical D, Polar Bear. And some will be quietly cooperative but not necessarily committed (yet!)—a typical S, Penguin. And there may be a small minority, whether they realise it or not—who will not be able to see themselves in the company's future.

Thinking Forward

Managing these changes in the transformation of the organisation sets the stage for an organisation that will be able to grow now and into the future, no matter what weather system rolls in. This requires effective communication strategies for all four behavioural styles, a confirmation of right people in the right seats, which sometimes requires shifting in personnel and/or training. When you take the time to move beyond quick fixes to designing healthy relationships that can cope well with transition and/or transformations, you position your organisation to be flexible and adaptable enough to respond effectively to anything the future holds.

Weather systems do not change the core values or the high dream of an organisation; they just adjust the means and methods of getting there. That's why organisations with an aligned workforce weather change the best; everyone is able to stay confident and encouraged through all kinds of transitions and weather systems.

Communications

Many Leaders operate on the basis of trial and error when it comes to interacting with their teams. The Carnegie Institute found that only 15% of success was due to technical skills, while 85% of success was due to people skills. Leaders have the opportunity to give themselves a huge advantage, because many organisations overlook this very important fact. We must become as skilled at developing relationships as we are at adapting to new technologies. The ability to understand and lead people comes from understanding personality styles in order to communicate and connect more effectively; building bridges not walls.

At the Acculturate phase this is critical. Working with your leadership team demands that we learn to communicate the purpose, values and strategy moving forward effectively – in a way that moves people to action. This knowledge will enable you to see the value each person possesses towards the success of your organisation. It gives you the choice (of which we are all at choice) to adapt your communications approach to achieve effective communication with others by "speaking their communication language."

The power of knowing who is a Polar Bear, Arctic Hare, Penguin or Leopard Seal will enable you to target their abilities to produce maximum results. Tips for communicating with the four behavioural styles are below:

WITH **D**'s	WITH **I**'s	WITH **S**'s	WITH **C**'s
Show them how to win	Show them that you admire and like them	Show them how your idea minimises risk	Approach indirectly, non-threatening
Display reasoning	Be optimistic	Demonstrate interest in them	Show your reasoning, or logic, give data in writing
Provide concise data	Support their feelings and ideas	Compliment them on follow through	Allow them to think, inquire and check before they make decisions
Agree on goals and boundaries	Avoid in-volved details	Give personal assurances	
Vary routine	Focus on the big picture	Provide a relaxing, friendly stable atmosphere	Tell them "why" and "how"
Compliment them on what they have done	Interact and participate with them– do it together	Act non-aggressively, focus on common interests	Provide opportunities for the precision, accuracy and planning for results
Provide opportunities for them to lead, impact results	Provide acknowl-edgements, accolades and compliments	Provide opportunities for deep contribution and teamwork	

Finding the Right Place

Sometimes during the Acculturate phase you will encounter people who are right for the organisation, but need to change positions to be properly aligned. This can mean promoting from within, moving people laterally, or even moving people out of leadership if they are ill-suited to its required tasks. Staying true to the core values and the relationship design is the key to making these transitions smooth and healthy.

The classic example of the position mismatch is the stellar salesperson who gets promoted into management. Sometimes this works, but other times the superstar who was breaking every company sales record does not do as well at supervising others. More often than not, the salesperson-turned-manager gets frustrated and bored, and the people he or she supervises start feeling resentful. The best move for the company is not to let the individual go, but to move him or her out of management and back into sales.

People who align well with the high dream, company purpose and values, but not with their current roles and responsibilities, will likely need help discovering a position for which they are better suited. As a leader, you need to take a look at their strengths and weaknesses and at the needs of the organisation. Consider where their talents are best suited to further the company's goals and give them an opportunity to grow. Sometimes you might even consider creating a new position for someone.

Employees are human beings, not robots who can be plugged in somewhere at random and function well. They perform best when they can put their heart and soul into what they do. And a company that treats its employees like human beings is much more likely to have employees that treat co-workers as well as customers and clients with the same care. That's what happens when we engage the heart as well as the mind.

Time to Go

One of the most challenging parts of the Acculturate phase is addressing the reality that some of the people you have may not be able to align honestly with the High Dream and Purpose and/or Values of the organisation. This can of course be because of a poor attitude or incompetence, and often these individuals will try to wait you out to see if the change will last. But others can't align with the freshly articulated high dream because it's just not compatible with how they are wired. The company may simply not be a good fit for them. This may have always been the case, but it becomes clear after the direction and priorities of the company have been clearly spelled out for everyone to see and understand.

After having spent almost her entire career in the private sector, Susan was recruited for a public sector job by a Deputy Minister who wanted to make some changes. He wanted to run his particular section of the government much more like a private company—setting clear goals, making concrete plans, and examining KPI's on a regular basis and recognising and rewarding performance. He wanted to cultivate an environment of healthy competition and strive for excellence. Excited and intrigued, Susan took the position.

The boss was true to his word, and Susan loved her new job. Although it was a public sector position, her responsibilities aligned perfectly with her strengths and passions. Unfortunately, six months later—just as the department was in the middle of implementing many exciting plans—the Deputy Minister who had hired Susan was transferred. A new Deputy Minister was hired who did not share the same vision. Not that the new vision was right or wrong, just different from the original plan. When the new leader made his vision clear, Susan knew that what the section was doing and where it was headed, did not align with her fundamental aspirations to be able to make that difference she originally wanted to make. So she made the difficult decision to leave.

Susan's experience is not uncommon. Companies change leadership or get bought out by other companies. The market conditions may shift in a way that requires a complete restructuring or other drastic changes. Sometimes it is individuals themselves that change: few of us have the same goals and needs we did ten or twenty years ago.

All of these can be perfectly legitimate reasons why a particular individual is no longer a good fit for your company, and none of them mean that anyone has done anything wrong. Alignment isn't about right or wrong, it's about fitting the puzzle pieces together. And someone who doesn't fit in your puzzle right now may be a stellar fit somewhere else.

Remember, by this time, it is much clearer to everyone what the organisation stands for and what is important to its leadership. Most likely there will be a few people who will look at those things and will not be able to see themselves as part of it moving forward. Sometimes they will come to you on their own and bring the matter to your attention. But other times, you will need to address the issue.

This can be very tricky, as some, or even all, of the people in this situation may be people you genuinely like and care about. They may be competent, hardworking and personable. But if someone can't align properly with the company vision, it is best for the organisation and for the individual if the person moves on to other opportunities. Remember, tyres that are poorly aligned not only make driving more difficult; they also wear out more quickly.

Who stays and who goes should not be an emotional decision. It must be based on what is best for the organisation. You also can't risk the company becoming polarised again by not making the hard decisions required to get everyone on the same page.

Good Transitions

Letting people go or people choosing to go—whether due to alignment to the core values, passion for the job roles & responsibilities, and/or capability to perform —is naturally perceived as a negative event. When such departures are not handled properly, rumours begin circulating, and people become afraid for their jobs. If you don't clearly communicate what's going on, people will start making things up to fill the void. Before you know it, people that you intended to keep may be going out on interviews and leaving on their own.

But these transitions don't have to be negative. For example, professional sports teams cut and trade players all the time. As often as not, a player who struggled in one franchise will thrive in another. How the decision is perceived depends entirely on your communication strategy.

In fact, personnel transitions offer an extremely important test of your commitment to transparency and truthfulness. That is why it is essential to stay in front of the situation. Once rumours get going, you'll find it easier to put toothpaste back into a tube than to control the messages being sent all over the office. Come out and be straightforward with your employees from the very beginning. They may not always like what you have to say, but they will respect you much more if you are open and honest.

Organisational transition can be a mysterious process, but effective communication keeps it transparent. How you manage these changes is important, not just to those who leave but also to the people you retain. Personnel changes should be discussed with the individual first and then communicated to the company as a transition, not a punishment. Be clear about how the change impacts everyone involved.

On the other hand, harsh exits traumatise everyone who remains with the company. Not long ago, we worked with a company that handled some exits poorly, and everyone who stayed—the "survivors," as they were known—was terrified. They were all convinced that they were next, and lived in constant uncertainty. Furthermore, the way the exits were handled went against everything the leaders of the organisation said they stood for, so the trust of the employees was severely damaged.

The beauty of following our five stages to organisational transformation is that the departures can actually be affirming events. Making these transitions positive goes back to how you've designed the relationship and your communications moving forward. When you've gone through the previous phases successfully and designed a relationship of genuine transparency and openness, even letting someone go doesn't have to be uncomfortable or traumatic. People who feel seen and heard and valued, and who have honestly confronted their own shortcomings are much more receptive to a truthful conversation about where they fit in the company.

Both of us have had the experience of receiving thank you notes from people that have been terminated. Susan has three that she keeps in her desk to this day. These people wrote to thank her for giving them the push they needed to try something different and new. Not only were they not performing up to their employers' standards, they were letting themselves down as well. They needed a push to leave their comfort zones so they could do better work somewhere else.

Recruiting to fill the Gaps

Knowing where your organisation is and where it's headed is vital to recruiting, hiring, training and succession planning. Every person in the company has the power to shape the culture by contributing to it or undermining it. Do you hire the programmer with the degree from the most prestigious school or the one with similar knowledge and skill from a less prestigious school, but whose talent will align and contribute to the culture you are trying to build?

You can buy two computers with identical hardware—monitors, CPU's and keyboards—but what will determine the user experience is the software—the operating system, the word processor and so on. You are hiring people to do much more than just perform certain tasks: you are hiring their talent (thoughts, feelings and behaviours), knowledge and skill.

The ideal you are aiming for in your organisation is to surround yourself with the right people who occupy the right seats, a Jim Collins concept in his book "Good to Great". As we said a few times already, who do we hire, who stays, who moves seats, and who goes should not be an emotional decision. It must be based on what is best for the organisation. You also can't risk the company becoming polarised again by not making the hard decisions required to get everyone on the same page. So, how do you do that?

It's now time to introduce you to our **Alignment Check**™

NAME	VALUE #1	VALUE #2	VALUE #3	VALUE #4	VALUE #5	DESIRE	ABILITY	COMMITMENT

The Standard: ☐ ☐ ☐ ☐ ☐ ☐ ☐ ☐

Rating: ✓ ✓/x x

To download this tool, please visit: **www.pbpbooks.com/tools**

This Alignment Check™ is inspired by the People Analyser™ concept from Gino Wickman's book, Traction. Our Alignment Check™ tool enables you to assess your people, better interview for new hires, better performance manage and in a few cases, identify who should no longer be in the company.

RIGHT PEOPLE

How do you use this tool? Now that you have the company core values confirmed, you can clearly define what the "right people" are for your organisation. It is people who live your company values on a daily basis and foster them through consistent role modelling. It is the DNA of your company.

You will assess people by their consistent faithfulness to living out the values by giving them the following ratings:

Check (✓) He or she lives out that core value most of the time.

Check (✓/x) He or she lives out the value sometimes but not consistently.

Check (𝕏) He or she doesn't live out the core value regularly.

When you are analysing your people, it is critical to identify those values that are non-negotiable and must be a check (✓); those that can be inconsistent with a check (✓/x); and there should never be an 𝕏 on any values.

If there is an 𝕏, the question you have to ask yourself is, will he or she improve enough to meet the minimum standard? Most will, and some won't. For those who won't, we do recommend that you give this person an opportunity to improve by communicating what your expectations are moving forward and holding them accountable through effective performance management discussions.

RIGHT SEATS

In chapter 8 we talked about the importance of your people being able to have the freedom and supports to advance as far as their **D**esires, **A**bilities and **C**ommitment (DAC) will carry them. The seats are defined as the responsibilities and accountabilities of their role in the organisation. The Alignment Check™ tool guides you on whether or not the individual is in the right seat by assessing the above mentioned components: **D**esire, **A**bility, and **C**ommitment to the seat. Lets breakdown these three components one at a time.

Desire: This means they truly want this role. They have the will to perform this job through its ups and downs, no matter what. They look at problems to solve as opportunities rather than complaining about the role.

Ability: They have the mental, emotional, relationship, physical and spiritual (MERPS) capacity and the required intellect to do the job.

Commitment: They believe in the purpose and vision of the organisation and have an unwavering understanding and dedication to their role and how it aligns to the bigger picture.

An "𝒳" on any of these three means it's not the right seat for the person. If the "𝒳" is in the ability only, sometimes you can change to a " ✓/𝓍". If you are willing to invest the time and money it takes to develop that ability. You have to ask yourself if you have the luxury of that time.

Step 1—Do an Alignment Check™ with your leadership team.

Step 2—Have your leadership team do an Alignment Check™ with everyone in their team and bring it back to the leadership team for discussion and analysis.

Step 3—Use this tool in your performance review discussions throughout the year to give your people feedback on how they are doing. Make it relevant and become part of the language in your company.

Step 4—Use this tool when interviewing new candidates. Design your questions and your reference checks around the Alignment Check™.

Remember, the Vision, Purpose and Values belong to everyone. Everyone who truly shares that dream should feel like they have a bright future with the organisation.

Ultimately, aligning with the high dream is all about creating an environment where all the people thrive within the company. Good solid ICE™ benefits Polar Bears, Penguins, Leopard Seals and Artic

Hares regardless of their differences. And when you have the right people in the right place doing the right stuff, amazing things will follow!

If this book has taught you nothing else, we hope it has shown you that change is possible. No matter where your company is, if you are willing to put in the work and lead by example, you can build the culture you want and attract the people who want to be part of it. Take the lessons of this book and get started! And if you find you need support, don't hesitate to reach out to us. We'd love to help.

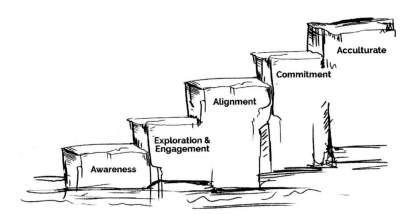

Image: 5 Step Roadmap to Acculturate

BONUS CHAPTER

. . . .

Putting the Principles and Rules of Engagement into Practice

Are you ready to Acculturate your organisation? So what should you do now? Hopefully we have ignited the passion and desire in you to raise the bar and begin the journey to becoming a high performing organisation.

CHAPTER 1:

Are you personally ready to embrace the diversity?

This chapter explains the four Guiding Principles which are essential for this journey to be successful:

1. **Be Committed**
2. **Be fully present with what is**
3. **Engage in deep dialogue**
4. **Believe that the answers are within**

We invite you to complete the Guiding Principles Assessment at the end of Chapter One to determine your leadership readiness to embrace diversity.

Is your Senior Leadership Team ready to embrace the diversity?

In terms of the effectiveness of a leadership team, our experience indicates that a team cohesiveness to these four guiding principles has far more impact on success than its level of experience or knowledge. In a few short words, being at least 75% strong in these principles is the biggest indicator of future success that your organisation can achieve in its transformation.

How do you Assess your team cohesiveness to these principles?

Collect the scores from each section as a team and identify the overall percentage strength for each principle knowing that you want to be at 75% or higher to be in the top quartile.Then ask the following questions for each principle:

1. What are you doing well as a team?
2. What do you need to be doing better as a team?
3. What do you need to stop doing?
4. What do you need to start doing?

CHAPTER 2:

State of The Relationships in Your Organisation?

Purpose: The purpose of this exercise is to gain awareness of relationships, employee aspirations, employee alignment to the organisation's aspirations and how much of their individual potential is being utilised.

Spend 15 minutes in a common area of your organisation (lobby, canteen etc.) being curious of everyone in the place. Without actually talking to anyone, be curious by asking yourself the following questions:

1. How are employees interacting with each other?

2. How are employees interacting with your customers?

3. What are their expressions?

4. How are they carrying themselves (body posture)?

5. How are they reacting to your presence?

6. What else is going on?

At the end of these 15 minutes capture your observations. Then spend some time over the coming days with 3 – 5 (or more) individuals from different parts from the organisation (preferably those who you are unfamiliar with), asking him or her these questions and see what you discover.

1. What is important to you?

2. What do you enjoy most about your work day?

3. What are your dreams?

4. What empowers you?

5. What is holding you back?

6. What are you missing in your work life?

7. What's important to you outside the office?

8. What part of your role fulfils you most?

9. What motivates you towards success?

10. What recognition do you like best?

11. What is your unique talent?

12. How would you describe your relationship at work?

Now ask yourself the following questions to reveal what behaviours are driving your organisation?

1. How does this person respond to you when you are curious?

2. What did you learn about being curious?

3. What behaviours are driving performance?

4. What company values are being honoured? Or not honoured?

5. How do you want to use this information in your organisation?

This is the beginning of having an **awareness** of what your organisation's culture is today and the strength of it. Is it what you need it to be for your company to be high performing? If it is what you need it to be, how strong is it? Will it survive possible threats (those unexpected weather systems that the radar didn't pick up)? Let's explore further to answer these questions.

CHAPTER 3:

How Strong is your ICE™?

The ICE™ of an organisation is its **I**nfrastructure, **C**onsciousness and **E**co-Wisdom™. These three areas form the environment of your organisational culture and determine its health and productivity. In a diverse organisation housing multiple personalities like the diversity of: polar bears, penguins, arctic hares and leopard seals - the strength of the ICE™ is key!

The cultural **infrastructure** of an organisation is reflected in the work routines and habits of its employees. What do employees do when they have a question about their job? How do they handle a problem with a customer or an altercation with a co-worker? What about when they have a new idea or a suggestion? How are they rewarded, acknowledged, and celebrated? What are the processes for growth? How does the ethnic diversity either enhance or inhibit each individual's self-expression? In summary, it is the channels through which authority, responsibility and communication flow.

A healthy infrastructure must strike the delicate balance between the primacy of the vision of the organisation and the importance of each individual within it. Are the employees of your company truly aligned with the vision? Do they believe they are an important part of bringing that vision to pass?

The **consciousness** of the organisation: How aware are individuals of how their words and actions affect others and the performance of the organisation as a whole? How does that awareness affect their behaviour?

The more developed the consciousness of an organisation, the more individuals will respect and appreciate each other's differences.

Leaders must first demonstrate the kind of consciousness they want to see in their organisation by effective empathic listening. This is the only way to encourage people to take the kind of risks necessary to get the full benefit of the wisdom housed in the organisation and nipping toxic behaviours in the bud. Do your employees feel comfortable communicating what they learn and challenging the status quo? Do they feel that they can do that at any time within appropriate, productive parameters?

Every species of animal has adapted to thrive in a particular ecosystem. This **"Eco-Wisdom™"** represents hundreds of thousands or even millions of years of accumulated information about how to interact with and thrive within the environment around them. Human culture is quite similar; people learn from birth how to interpret and respond to subtle facial expressions and all sorts of non-verbal cues. Early in life, we reach the point where we are able to formulate subtle complex responses to a variety of stimuli without even thinking.

Diverse organisations have a tremendous, often untapped, advantage when it comes to Eco-Wisdom™. Instead of two hundred employees who all understand how to interact with, manage and market to the inhabitants of one narrow region of one country, diverse organisations possess within them the potential to reach customers and markets all over the world.

The Eco-Wisdom™ of an organisation can be even greater than the sum of the wisdom of each individual when each is able to share with and learn from others. Harnessing this resource in a diverse company can produce teams of individuals who are uniquely adaptable to all different situations. Leaders who are able to engage with their employees and make the process fun, will encourage the kind of creativity and innovation that can ultimately drive the organisation far ahead of the competition.

How well is your organisation utilising its Eco-Wisdom™? Do employees have opportunities for personal and professional growth?

Become aware of the condition of your ICE™ by having all members of your leadership team take the "Get a feel for your ICE™" assessment at the end of chapter 3. If you truly believe the answers are within, we encourage you to take this assessment to all levels of leadership/ management in your organisation. To get a 100% assessment of your ICE™, you can engage your entire organisation in a more detailed annual assessment using the Gallup Q12 Employee Engagement Survey (www.q12.gallup.com) which can be self-administered.

Collect the scores from each section of ICE™ as a leadership team and identify the overall percentage strength for each component, knowing that you want to be at 80% or higher overall to be in the top quartile. Then ask the following questions for each component:

1. How strong is your Infrastructure? Consciousness? Eco-Wisdom™?

2. What cracks do you have in your ICE™?

3. What fissures do you have in your ICE™?

4. Where are the breaking points?

Have each division/department of your organisation facilitate this process with their leader/managers to gain further clarity on fissures, cracks and breaking points.

CHAPTER 4:

Get on your ICE™ to explore and engage with your Employees

Getting on the ICE™ is about taking responsibility for relationships within your leadership team and/or functional teams that could be healthier and thus more productive. Your journey will require some preparation and supplies. And just like no one thought the journey to the South Pole would be easy, it's best to give up the hope of a "quick fix" from the beginning and settle in for the long haul. A friendly reminder of one of the guiding principles—**Be Committed.**

Before engaging, you and the leaders of your organisation must assess the state of relationships and redesign them if necessary. Do people feel respected and valued? Do they know what to do when they feel upset or offended? What about when they have a good idea or a suggestion? Keep in mind during the exploration phase that most people just want to feel that they are being seen and heard. This may look and feel different in different cultures, but the human need is ultimately the same.

Rules on the ICE™

Remember, people don't leave or disengage with companies, they leave and/or disengage with Leaders.

Leaders, must take **responsibility for their impact** and manage it accordingly to bring out the best for those in relationship with them. In other words, they must understand how they are perceived by the diverse employee base of polar bears, penguins, arctic hares and the leopard seals.

The challenge facing diverse organisations is to allow all employees to be themselves while **"holding the focus"** on the organisation's purpose, vision and values. The good news is, that when the relationship is intentionally designed and leaders stay focused on the mission and vision, the ICE™ will remain strong in the face of challenges.

Be prepared to discuss the following questions with your employees:

1. Why does the organisation exist?

2. What are the fundamental values of your organisation?

3. What business are you in?

4. What are your dreams for the company?

5. What is the plan to get there?

6. How does their job impact the above?

7. What makes your organisation better than the competition?

The way to find out what is really going on is to ask powerful questions, which support the guiding principle of **"deep dialogue."** These questions are like the sled dogs in your arctic exploration: they will take you where you need to go.

Asking **powerful questions** requires a level of emotional intelligence, but that can be learned and developed by leaders. When asking powerful questions, it's important to be willing to gently bend a few polar bear and penguin taboos with the goal of forging a new workplace culture where everyone can be open about the things that are important to the success of the organisation as well as to the individual. This can be done in a way that isn't perceived as rude but rather as liberating: giving people permission to express how they really feel.

One of the most powerful ways to engage your polar bears, penguins, arctic hares and leopard seals is to ask them to complete this sentence:

"I work best when…"

This is an open-ended inquiry that gently encourages your employees to consider what they need in order to be productive. What do they need in order to do their job well? The flip side of the question indirectly forces the employee to consider which aspects of productivity are his or her own responsibilities. If I have what I need, what should I be producing?

Other powerful questions include:

- What is working well for you right now?

- What is keeping you awake at night?

- If you could change just one thing about work, what would it be?

- What are relationships like in the workplace right now for you? Do you have friends there?

- How excited are you to get up in the morning and come to work?

Sometimes questions with calibrated answers can help employees express their feelings more accurately:

- On a scale of 1-10, how fulfilled are you in your job right now?"

- What would a 10 look like for you?

Not all powerful questions have to come in response to a crisis or even a challenge. Some of the best questions to ask on an ongoing basis include:

- What can we improve?

- How can we grow?

The key to these kinds of powerful questions is to ask them in a spirit of genuine curiosity.

Employees will sense this and respond with accurate, honest descriptions of what they feel, not justifications for what they think or do. Judgement will be received with defensiveness, but curiosity will often be received with genuine helpfulness and openness.

For an extensive list of powerful questions to assist you in this exploration please refer to the exercise at the end of this chapter.

Powerful questions are all well and good. However, if the leader is not prepared to **listen well** (without interrupting/judgement/repercussions/reprisals) to the employee, the interaction may do more harm than good. Listening well is not only listening to the words that are said, it is everything from people's facial expressions and body language to the heaviness of the air in the room. **Listening well is when you know it's time to ask** "What is it that isn't being said right now?"

Listening well is powerful. Over and over, we have observed that if leaders are committed to listening well during the explore and engagement phase, the atmosphere of the room softens and people open up. The dialogue gets deeper and lasting trust is built.

We invite you to complete the Relationship Design tool at the end of this chapter. This tool is about taking responsibility for relationships within your leadership team and/or functional team that could be healthier and thus more productive. If listening well is an area of opportunity for you please refer to the levels of listening exercises following the Relationship Design Tool.

CHAPTER 5:

What is the POOP™ in your organisation and how to dispose of it?

P— Preconceived ideas

O—Obstacles

O—Obsessions

P— Prejudices

During the exploration and engagement phase, you will have uncovered underlying polarity and toxicity. You can minimise the negative effects by addressing the issues you discover right away. It means getting engaged in the POOP™ and articulating it, so you can then do something with it. Otherwise it will just stink and become toxic!

You will be investigating the sources of toxicity as well as any negative baggage that people have from previous attempts at change. Sometimes you will discover that people feel that they have offered input and suggestions in the past and that no one listened to what they said or nothing was done. Regardless of what you find in your exploration, remember that the productive reaction to any negative indicator is not panic but **genuine curiosity.**

All of us bring **preconceived ideas** to work with us, and these tend to vary greatly by culture. Preconceived ideas are not wrong in and of themselves. The problem comes when we fail to recognise and critically examine them.

Preconceived ideas often cover the grey areas of behaviour such as the way we demonstrate courtesy and respect. Polar bears may consider it rude if you fail to bow to a new acquaintance, but penguins may be comfortable kissing someone on the cheek when they first meet. Part of playing in the POOP™—preconceived ideas is to determine where they may be causing unnecessary conflict and polarity.

Take a few quiet moments alone and ask **yourself** the following questions to become aware of your preconceived ideas:

1. What's the image that you hold of your organisation?

2. How do others see the organisation's capabilities?

3. What other ideas, thoughts and feelings do you have about your organisation?

4. What's the image you hold of your team?

5. How do you see their capabilities?

6. What other ideas, thoughts and feelings do you have about this team/organisation?

Are any of your thoughts from above causing unnecessary conflict and polarity? What about others on your team? How would they answer these questions?

The **obstacles** in POOP™, however, are the personal challenges that prevent individuals from doing their jobs well and reaching their goals. These can include everything from the attitude they bring to work to any challenges they may face involving fear, anxiety or even depression. Other personal obstacles could include skill or educational deficiencies or other professional needs. Begin cataloguing the obstacles you uncover so that you can strategise how to help individuals overcome them.

Take a few quiet moments alone and ask **yourself** the following questions to become aware of your obstacles:

1. What challenges are getting in the way of people doing their jobs well?

2. What seems to be the some fears in the organisation? What seem to be the main fears in the organisation?

3. What's not being said?

4. What concerns you the most about...?

5. What is holding your organisation back?

6. What are some of the barriers?

If you have obstacles in your way, how can you overcome them? What obstacles are in the way for others on your leadership team?

An inclination or a preference becomes an obsession when the person in question is unable to bend on an issue when circumstances require it. Diverse organisations need a certain degree of flexibility from everyone if they are to flourish. Take careful note of any obsessions you uncover during the exploration phase, so that they can be handled directly and sensitively.

Take a few quiet moments alone and ask yourself the following questions to become aware of your obsessions:

1. What are we hanging onto?

2. What are we intolerant to?

3. What are we not prepared to let go of?

4. If you could wipe the slate clean what would you do?

5. What's really important for you right now?

6. What's important about that?

7. What are the drivers behind that?

What Obsessions might you be holding on to? What about others on your leadership team?

All human beings bring **prejudices** to the table. These may include assumptions about management, co-workers and even the organisation itself. Most people have been repeatedly told that prejudice is wrong, whether in school or in a business setting. Unfortunately, this has led many to believe they must deny having any prejudices at all, rather than admitting them and examining them critically. Do your best to create a non-judgmental, comfortable space where people can admit their prejudices on their own.

Take a few quiet moments alone and ask **yourself** the following questions to become aware of your prejudices:

1. What have you made up about people on your team?

2. What judgement have you formulated?

3. What are the beliefs around this?

4. What are you tolerating?

After careful examination of prejudices you or others on your leadership team may have, how can you work through them?

Daniel Goleman stating that "understanding what is going on is only part of a healthy relationship, it is what you do with it, that really matters". How you respond to your own POOP™ observations and what you hear from others in your organisation in this stage of the journey will be a make or break to the desired transformation. There is no room for judging, repercussions or reprisals. This exploration is done with a spirit of **genuine curiosity.**

Communication styles that can predict the end of a relationship - Rather than confronting the POOP™ (which tends to accumulate!) with our employees, we can make evasive manoeuvres such as tuning out, turning away, acting busy, or engaging in obsessive behaviours.

Being able to identify The Four Horsemen, which we refer to as the Four Toxic Behaviours in this book (blame, defensiveness, contempt, stonewalling), is a necessary first step to eliminating them, but this knowledge is not enough. To drive away destructive communication patterns, you must replace them with healthy, productive ones.

What can you do if you notice yourself participating in or being subjected to criticism, defensiveness, contempt, and/or stonewalling? Refer to the step by step proven process to turn the situation/conversation into a healthy productive one.

Emotional management is one of the most difficult skills to master as a leader and in teams because most of the members of any team are not always comfortable managing their emotions publicly or discussing emotions in a group setting. It requires a commitment from the leadership team to work together to spot when emotions are steering their progress or lack thereof. The goal is to interact effectively with one another. Without this, toxic behaviours can creep into this journey, causing a major weather system and devastating damage in its aftermath.

We highly recommend that you and your leadership team take the time to explore your readiness for this part of the journey by taking the Emotional Intelligence (EQ) assessment at the end of this chapter to have an awareness of self and your impact on others.

Cleaning up after you have collected all the POOP™ in the room is messy business. It takes time, patience, and heart—as you test emotions and push boundaries. But only by bringing to the surface and deliberating over undiscussables can we ensure our teams operate to their full potential.

CHAPTER 6:

The Dream for your organisation

There's an old saying that if you don't know where you're going, any road will take you there. Aligning with the high dream is all about knowing exactly where you're going and being fully **committed** to the journey. It's about more than running away from the POOP™; it's about running toward the best.

The high dream is not just about what you desire to accomplish, but also whom you are being while you are accomplishing. The values of the organisation, as well as its goals, start to emerge. The **ICE™** is thick and smooth, meaning that the Infrastructure, Consciousness and Eco-Wisdom™ are strong. This allows both polar bears and penguins to thrive, as the organisation's core values connect with the personal values of each team member.

We invite you to do an exercise with your leadership team to get them excited about what's possible for you and your organisation. This is at the end of this chapter. Remember, this is truly a brainstorming, fun, engaging and creative beginning to the next phase of the process. It is recommended it is done in an off-site, casual and neutral environment. **This is not replacing or creating the Purpose, Mission or Vision. It is truly taking a deep breath now that we have gotten rid of the POOP™, our voices have been heard and we all want the BEST for the organisation.**

The key to effective alignment is the power of being **at choice.** Not only do we articulate what we want for ourselves and for the organisation, we articulate what we can do to get to what we want. This means we take responsibility for facilitating the change we want to see, and we feel empowered to bring it about. When everyone in your organisation can articulate clearly what the high dream is, they are more easily able to consciously choose to align or not.

Alignment in your organisation is a similar concept. You are not achieving alignment by making a polar bear into a penguin or vice versa. You are merely adjusting the connection between each person and the organisation itself. Diverse organisations have to stretch further to achieve alignment, but the opportunity for growth is also greater.

Staying aligned to the high dream for your organisation requires a deeper understanding of the day to day challenges departments face. At your next leadership team meeting, create an environment where each functional head can share safely their challenges, struggles and frustrations of daily life in that function/department. This requires people to be fully transparent, open and tolerant where everyone honours and appreciates the current reality without judgement or POOP™. Once shared, the group is then asked the following questions:

1. What's the most important thing you just heard?

2. What are the challenges and pressures?

3. How does this department/role need help and support?

4. What is needed to be fully aligned?

5. How do we hold each other accountable to the needs?

Ultimately, aligning with the high dream involves an individual commitment to transparency, openness and tolerance. It also requires a group commitment to honouring and appreciating one another's contributions. As each of us strives to be the best we can be, we build something so much greater together.

CHAPTER 7:

Defining and/or Refining your culture

To lead a diverse organisation effectively requires patience, tenacity and a heart level commitment to the principles we've outlined in the previous chapters. It takes genuine concern for the people you lead and work with. But when those qualities are authentically present, they are shockingly contagious. They begin to spread organically to the rest of the organisation even beyond the intentional efforts of the leadership.

You can build a work culture that is so powerful that it draws all your employees into the right behaviours and discourages them from the behaviours that don't serve. The environment of your company can be so positive that everyone wants to be a part of it. And before long, the behaviours you are looking for become second nature.

Because all human beings are imperfect, we need accountability in order to live our best lives. Left to our own devices, we may deviate from all that we can be. The organisational culture you worked so hard to build is made up of imperfect individuals who are no exception to this rule; they too need accountability to thrive. Our default behaviours are not necessarily harmonious, so we have to help one another along to ensure we don't slip back into our old ways.

The best form of accountability is conspicuously living out the values of the organisation, starting with the leadership team itself. It is this ongoing, consistent behaviour from leadership that creates and reinforces the cultural norms of the organisation. From there, it is natural to affirm others who are doing the same, and, when necessary, correct or adjust those who fail to do so. The key to this feedback being meaningful is the correlation of their behaviour rightly or wrongly, to the core values.

To develop, validate or refine your organisation's core values, facilitate the exercise at the end of this chapter with the leadership team. As a gentle reminder, this is NOT a task to be delegated!

Why do we all come to work every day, beyond the pay cheque? Ultimately, the behaviours we value are rooted in the purpose and high dream for the organisation. When people truly buy-in and see how their roles contribute to that higher purpose, they will be motivated to do a great job.

Now take a few minutes to think/rethink/confirm your organisation's reason for being. As Harry Beckwith once said "People don't lead, purposes do".

Consider these questions:

What is your organisation's core purpose (mission statement)? - In other words, when your employees are on their way to work every day, what do you want them to be saying is their purpose? For example, we know Disney employees come to work to make people happy. Google's employees come to work every day to organise the world's information and make it universally accessible and useful and Walmart employees help people save money so they can live better.

The commonality between these three is what makes up a good purpose statement. Every employee can see their role and responsibilities within it. As a leadership team, start answering the following questions to identify what your organisational purpose is:

1. What do we do?

2. What makes us different?

3. For whom do we do it?

4. Why does our organisation's existence matter?

5. What is our most important reason for being here? Why?

6. What would be lost if this organisation ceased to exist?

7. Why are we important to the people we serve?

8. Why would anyone dedicate their precious time, energy, and passion to our company? (Note: the answer is not money.)

Defining your core purpose is all about clarity, authenticity, and alignment. This means that you do not have to sound "sexy." This is not something that has to sound impressive on a billboard. It does, however, have to feel meaningful. You'll know when you finally identify your core purpose because it will be accompanied by a strong sense of conviction. The team will feel a deep "yes!" when it is uncovered.

The work culture, as embraced and lived out by each leader and employee, is organic. It will be both reaffirmed and refined over time. As the needs of your organisation change, there may be corresponding changes in the culture. This means that we don't need to feel pressured to get it perfect right away.

Lastly, we want your employees to know your BHAG. What is a BHAG? A Big Hairy Audacious Goal is a statement of Strategic Intention—the specific result the organisation will achieve in 10-30 years time. It is the inspiring "Mount Everest" they will climb. It is one of the components of the company's high dream.

Why is it useful? It is a very powerful way to communicate a clear direction and level of ambition that aligns the whole organisation. The leadership team must be committed to the BHAG, or it will not only have no power, it will reduce credibility.

What is the BHAG for your organisation?

Chapter 8:

Embrace Diversity

The high dream, purpose, values and BHAG belong to everyone in the company, not just the CEO. Within the world of that high dream, it is essential that everyone feels they are free to advance as far as their Desire, Ability and Commitment will carry them.

By now, you have a lot of good ideas about how to begin to build bridges between polar bears and penguins. But people don't differ only by roles and responsibilities, culture or ethnicity. Every human being is different from every other. We all have our own distinct fingerprints, signatures and DNA profiles. In addition to being an original combination of genetic material, every person on earth has had a unique combination of experiences and relationships. So even in a culturally homogenous organisation, there is a tremendous diversity of personalities and preferences.

One of the most useful ways to think about these individual differences is by understanding the patterns of behaviour that we exhibit when confronted with typical situations. As individuals, how do we deal with problems and challenges? With people and contacts? With preferred pace and level of consistency? And, with procedures and constraints?

Contrary to popular belief, a high performing culture is not one that is always conflict-free. It's really easy to avoid conflict by surrounding yourself with people who share your temperament and preferences, or who just accept without being fully committed, but that is not necessarily the best way to build a high performing organisation.

Nearly a century ago, Dr. William Moulton Marston introduced the concept of the DISC personality profile, focusing on behaviour tendencies that were directly observable. Unlike many other psychological theories rooted in abstractions, DISC was developed for a very practical reason: to help people manage their relationships more effectively and embrace diversity.

Effective leaders recognise that various personality styles are expressed differently in different environments. The classic DISC profile is a needs-motivated profile which measures energy put into how you deal with problems and challenges, how you deal with people and contacts, how you deal with pace and consistency and procedures and constraints. It measures people's emotions, needs and fears.

DISC is **NOT** a measure of intelligence, skills, education or experience or an indicator of values. DISC is a combination of nature (inherent) and nurture (learnt). The DISC model describes four different styles: Dominance (D), Influence (I), Steadiness (S) and Conscientiousness (C), All of us possess all four components in some measure, but usually one or two tend to govern the way we prefer to work. No style is right or wrong, but people with each style tend to have certain strengths, needs and weaknesses. By learning more about each, we learn more about ourselves, our co-workers and those who makes up our organisation

To Embrace Diversity, awareness of self is needed first. What are you? Are you a D (Polar Bear), I (Arctic Hare), S (Penguin) or C (Leopard Seal)? Take the DISC profile and learn more about self by visiting **www.pbpbooks.com**.

Once you know self, you will be in a better position to adapt to other DISC styles. Once the team engages in their own DISC profiles you can engage in team building with this new-found awareness.

You will find all four of the DISC styles in your organisation and in different parts of yourself. Sometimes you may feel that your style varies by situation or setting. Someone might be a D at work but more of an I at home, for example. The point of utilising these kinds of tools is that awareness of these differences empowers you as a leader to understand yourself and your people better. The goal in becoming educated about the styles is not to make excuses for yourself by saying, "Oh, I'm a D. That's just how I react to these things." Instead, growing leaders will use their knowledge and understanding of the styles to consider their own strengths and weaknesses and to better relate to their co-workers and direct reports and take responsibility for their impact.

By making the choice to be aware and adapt, leaders can work on the best ways to strengthen communication with each other. After you and your leadership team take the assessment, ask the following questions in a relaxed team environment . We encourage you to take this as a team building opportunity outside of the workplace environment:

Allow the team to one-by-one respond to the below questions:

1. When I'm working on a project or plan I prefer…

2. I am motivated when…

3. When working in a team environment I…

4. When I am emotionally charged / or someone on my team gets emotionally charged I…

5. I get frustrated most when…

6. What I most appreciate from others on my team is…

7. When problem solving I need most…

Asking these few simple yet powerful questions and through observation, you and your leaders can gain a greater understanding of your employees. Adapting your style is not always easy; it takes time, practice and patience. For tools and techniques on how to identify the diversity on your team and adapt and communicate with other styles, please refer to the chapter.

CHAPTER 9:

Alignment Check™ to leverage the Eco-Wisdom™

Once your team is beginning to align with the high dream, purpose and values, you can begin to truly leverage the "Eco-Wisdom™" of your organisation. This is where you start to see significant payout on the investment you have put in during the earlier stages. For diverse organisations, this is the stage where what might have been your greatest weakness becomes your greatest strength.

When you are in the habit of engaging both the hearts and minds of your employees, you encourage everyone to not only be on task but to be "on purpose" every day. As the high dream is gaining momentum, you will probably see a mixture of reactions: some will instantly feel motivated, anticipating all the exciting developments on the horizon—a typical I, Arctic Hare. Others will feel anxious and apprehensive, not sure of what to expect—a typical C, Leopard Seal. Other will just want to get going and get on with getting the job done—a typical D, Polar Bear. And some will be quietly cooperative but not necessarily committed (yet!)—a typical S, Penguin. *And there may be a small minority, whether they realise it or not—who will not be able to see themselves in the company's future.*

In the transformation of your organisation it is important that it will be able to grow now and into the future, no matter what weather system rolls in. This requires effective communication strategies for all four behavioural styles and a confirmation that you have the right people in the right seats.

Sometimes during the Acculturate phase you will encounter people who are right for your organisation, but need to change positions to be properly aligned. This can mean promoting from within, moving people laterally, or even moving people out of leadership if they are ill-suited to its required tasks. Staying true to the core values and the relationship design is the key to making these transitions smooth and healthy.

Who stays, who moves seats and who goes should not be an emotional decision. It must be based on what is best for the organisation. You also can't risk the company becoming polarised again by not making the hard decisions required to get everyone on the same page.

The Alignment Check™ introduced in this final chapter removes the emotion and ensures that you have the right people in the right seats doing the right stuff. To download this tool, please visit **www. pbpbooks.com**.

You can self implement many of the concepts we have talked about in this book and we would love to personally work with you and your team for you to gain maximum benefit from this methodology and facilitate implementation within your organisation.

To find out more, simply go online at **www.pbpbooks.com**.

Let's get started, are you ready?!

ACKNOWLEDGEMENTS

. . . .

This book is the product of many years of experience we have gained through working with individuals, teams and companies in many different countries and cultures.

We share a passion for helping organisations and people be the best they can be. What we do know is that people are emotional first and rational second. We also know employees and customers must be emotionally engaged in order for the organisation to be high performing.

We want to thank all of our clients over the years who entrusted us to take them on a journey that didn't have a clear path, but rather a solid foundation of principles that enabled us to explore even the most uncomfortable territories.

A PERSONAL THANK YOU
from Kevin

. . . .

This book is a result of a true team effort. Carl Gould and I were having lunch at a lovely local restaurant in Manama, Kingdom of Bahrain back in October 2013. Carl was in Bahrain to give a learning event to Entrepreneur Organisation (EO), of which I was the learning chair for the local chapter at that time. As we were enjoying the delightful food, quaint ambiance and temperate climate he asked me about the work I had been doing with organisations and leaders in the Middle East region. As he listened intently a far cry from his homeland environment of USA, he suddenly blurted, "that sounds like Polar Bears and Penguins". Referring to the challenging circumstances I discussed with him...In essence Polar Bears and Penguins occupy similar territory yet they know little about each other. Hence the book Polar Bears and Penguins was born!

I would also like to thank all the people over the years that have challenged me and allowed me to grow as a leader. From the early days of my career at the John Lewis Partnership where I was introduced to the skills of coaching and leadership by David Wilson and his team, and all those I worked with at DHL for six years learning the art of activity behind high performance, and to all my clients who unbeknown to them have impacted my growth as a person. To CTI's faculty leaders of the Leadership programme (Karen and Pat) for inviting my transformation, albeit painful at times, allowing me to claim my authenticity and to the coach training leaders for encouraging me to continue to open and lead from my heart with compassion and fierce courage. And to my EO Forum who have been there for me through the good and not so good times championing my learning & growth and to leave a legacy—thank you.

A PERSONAL THANK YOU
from Susan

. . . .

An undertaking such as this would never happen without inspiration. It all began for me when I joined Canadian Pacific Hotels & Resorts many years ago. The leaders, Robert DeMone, Carolyn Clark and Peter Watson to name just a few of the many, truly understood and lived the culture of engagement long before that word became common language.

I continue to be inspired by the work of The Gallup Organisation and Gino Wickman, the creator of The Entrepreneurial Operating System® (EOS®). The principles and beliefs when joined together create a dynamic transformation for even the most dysfunctional teams and organisations into one of a high performing culture. It is mesmerising when it unfolds.

To my friends and family who continuously said to me "Susan, you must write a book". You know who you are! Thank you! It took a while and a push from my business partner Kevin to make it happen.

To Larry, my husband, who continually believed in me and supported me through thick and thin. I thank you from the bottom of my heart.

A PERSONAL THANK YOU
from Us Both

. . . .

To Julia Nelson, thank you for making this book readable and educational! Sue Addison for dotting the "I's" and crossing the "T's" and Kendra Cagle for all of your wonderful graphics. We love the animals.

To the Coaches Training Institute (CTI), Johan Premfors and all our faculty leaders for giving us the courage to enter the danger zone in order to evoke transformation for ourselves and our clients.

And finally to our co-author Carl, who for which this book would never be revealed or happened; keeping us on track and guiding us every step of the way

We are extremely grateful for your wisdom, insights and support in bringing this book into reality—Thank you

ABOUT THE AUTHORS

....

Kevin and Susan started GRIP Arabia in 2015 to bring about a holistic approach to building a high performing organisation. Together they help business leaders on the journey of a high performing culture through engagement; for them to truly get a grip on their organisational culture and achieve results!

....

Kevin Craig

Kevin has a passion for growing leaders and helping organisations be their best. His work results in shifting high performing individuals, leaders and their organisational cultures to responsibility, accountability and capability.

Kevin formed Craig Consultants and Marketing in 2008. He has partnered with thousands of leaders and teams from both international & national organisations. His passion lies in working with influential leaders who are hungry to learn and grow. Craig Consultants was awarded "Best Executive Coaching Company—Middle East" by GCC Excellence Awards 2017. Kevin himself was named and awarded the "Best 100 Global Coaching Leaders" Award by World Coaching & HRD Congress & CHRO Asia in 2017.

Kevin's fierce courage and engaging personality enable his clients to go to the next level as he challenges them with tough love, all in service of them being at their best.

Kevin has always enjoyed starting and running businesses, expanding his skills and experiences. His most recent venture, GRIP Arabia is testament to his passion about growing and connecting people to both head and heart, to live truly fulfilled lives.

Kevin is a Certified Professional Co-active Coach (CPCC), Professional Certified Coach (PCC) with the International Coaching Federation (ICF), and global Faculty Leader for the Coaches Training Institute (CTI), with over 10,000 hours facilitation and coaching. He is an active member of EO (Entrepreneurs Organisation) Bahrain Chapter and certified forum facilitator for both EO & YPO (Young Presidents Organisation). Kevin was recently named and awarded the "Best 100 Global Coaching Leaders" by CHRO Asia, a testament to his competence.

LinkedIn: https://www.linkedin.com/in/kevinscraig/

. . . .

Susan Stevenson

Susan is a co-founder of GRIP Arabia, a company based in the Kingdom of Bahrain focusing on enabling organisations and individuals to realise their full potential and positively impact their desired business results. She is also an International Implementer of The Entrepreneurial Operating System®, helping SME's get what they want out of their businesses. EOS combines timeless business principles with a set of simple, practical, real-world tools to help entrepreneurs get what they want from their businesses.

Susan is an experienced senior level executive with over 20 years experience in a multicultural professional environment. She has worked in the Middle East, Europe, North America, United Mexican States, Bermuda and Barbados for international hotel companies, 4-5 star restaurants, golf resorts, retail, financial, aviation, logistics, and telecoms sectors. Her passion for developing people and organizations has enabled her to focus on being a catalyst to changes that deliver outstanding results and sustainability.

Susan graduated in Business Administration from her hometown university in Prince Edward Island, Canada. Susan is a professional trained Co-Active Coach with Coaches Training Institute and has been living in the Middle East since 2005 with her husband Larry and their five dogs.

LinkedIn: https://www.linkedin.com/in/suejstevenson/

. . . .

Carl Gould

Carl Gould is a business growth expert who advises organisations in order for them to get to the next level. He is a serial entrepreneur who built three multi-million dollar businesses by age 40. Gould created the world's farthest-reaching mentoring programme, and his methodologies are in practice in 35 countries.

Carl is a best-selling author, authoring books on the subject of business strategy, leadership and personal growth. He co-hosts "Quit and Get Rich", a weekly radio programme; and shares his insights from working with top organisations from around the world. Carl is married with three children, and lives in New Jersey, USA.

SERVICES AVAILABLE

. . . .

Polar Bears and Penguins has a number of programmes it offers its clients and is owned by GRIP Arabia W.L.L.; a full-service leadership-consulting organisation, located in Manama, Kingdom of Bahrain. It was founded in 2015 by Kevin Craig and Susan Stevenson with its motto of "Get a grip".

Some of the services we offer are:

- Assessments
- Organisational consulting
- Values based business planning
- Culture design
- Internal engagement
- Leadership team Alignment Checks™
- Leadership development
- Embracing diversity
- Executive/Leadership Coaching
- Retreat facilitation
- Speaking engagements

For further information on the *Polar Bears and Penguins* and GRIP Arabia W.L.L. and its activities and programmes, please contact:

- *Polar Bears and Penguins* book*:* **www.pbpbooks.com**
- GRIP Arabia W.L.L.: **www.GRIPArabia.com**

Introduction

The story of the American President visiting Australia in 1992, then American President, George H.W. Bush came from *apnewsarchive.com*.

CANBERRA, AUSTRALIA CANBERRA, Australia (AP) _ President Bush gave the V-for-victory sign as he drove in his armored limousine past some demonstrators in Australia's capital.

A friendly gesture?

Not down under. In Australia, holding up two fingers to form a "V" has the same meaning as a middle-finger salute in the United States.

It's not clear if Bush had been apprised of the local customs before his passing encounter.

That same day, at the opening of an Australian Center for American Studies, Bush noted that while the two cultures share much in common, "differences do exist. And we can and should do much more to foster greater understanding."

Guiding Principles

Travis Bradberry and Jean Greaves, *The Emotional Intelligence Quick Book,* (New York: Simon & Schuster, 2005)

Powerful questions is a term introduced in a book by Henry Kimsey-House, Karen Kimsey-House and Phillip Sandahl, *Co-Active Coaching: Changing Business Transforming Lives* (Nicholas Brealey, 2011)

Awareness of Your ICE™

The connection between culture, cockpit communication and plane crashes is from Malcolm Gladwells book, *Outliers* (Little Brown and Company, 2008)

Gallup's employee engagement work is based on more than 30 years of in-depth behavioral economic research involving more than 17 million employees. Through rigorous research, Gallup has identified 12 core elements—the Q12—that link powerfully to key business outcomes. Available online at http://www.gallup.com

Rules of Engagement

Understanding is only part of a relationship; it is what you do with it that really matters is in a book by Daniel Goleman, *Emotional Intelligence: Why It Can Matter More Than IQ,* (New York: Bantam, 2005)

Powerful questions exploration, adapted with approval, Coaches Training Institute, Co-Active Coaching: Changing Business Transforming Lives, (Boston: Nicholas Brealey, 2011). Available on line at www.coactive.com/learning-hub/intermediate/fulfillment/res/tools/FUL-Sample-Powerful-Questions.pdf

The two aspects of Listening, awareness and intuition are articulated through the 3 Levels of Listening from *Co-Active Coaching: Changing Business Transforming Lives,* (Boston: Nicholas Brealey, 2011). For further information it is available on line at http://www.coactive.com/learning-hub/fundamentals/res/FUN-Topics/FUN-Co-Active-Coaching-Skills-Listening.pdf

Getting Rid of Toxic Waste

Understanding is only part of a relationship; it is what you do with it that really matters is in a book by Daniel Goleman, *Emotional Intelligence: Why It Can Matter More Than IQ,* (New York: Bantam, 2005)

The Four Horsemen of the Apocalypse is a metaphor depicting the end of times in the New Testament. They describe conquest, war, hunger, and death respectively. Dr. Gottman uses this metaphor to describe communication styles that can predict the end of a relationship. His metaphor can be viewed on line at https://www.gottman.com/blog/the-four-horsemen-recognizing-criticism-contempt-defensiveness-and-stonewalling/

The EQ Assessment was adapted from the San Diego City College MESA Program which is available online at http://www.sdcity.edu/portals/0/cms_editors/mesa/pdfs/emotionalintelligence.pdf

The Johari Window is a communication model that is used to improve understanding between individuals. The word "Johari" is taken from the names of Joseph Luft and Harry Ingham, who developed the model in 1955. Using this tool to improve communications with you and your team is taken from the Educational Business Article, http://www.educational-business-articles.com/johari-window/

The case study, "Appreciation is Greater", adapted from the book by Kyle Idleman, *Grace is Greater,* (Baker: Grand Rapids, 2017)

Aligning Around The High Dream

The refrain "If you don't know where you're going, any road'll take you there" was a paraphrase of an exchange between Alice and the Cheshire Cat in Chapter 6 of Lewis Carroll's book, Alice's Adventures in Wonderland: "Would you tell me, please, which way I ought to go from here?"

The high dream is inspired from the brief, *Introduction to Process Work Theory*, by Stanford Siver, 2005

Define Your Culture

"Culture eats strategy for breakfast," is a famous quotation attributed to the late business management guru Peter Drucker, and articulated in the Shep Hypen article: Drucker Said *'Culture Eats Strategy For Breakfast' And Enterprise Rent-A-Car Proves It.* Can be viewed on line at www.forbes.com/sites/shephyken/2015/12/05/drucker-said-culture-eats-strategy-for-breakfast-and-enterprise-rent-a-car-proves-it/#1999d3572749

Make your values mean something, Patrick M Lencioni Harvard Business Review, July 2002

People don't lead, purposes do! is a quote from Harry Beckwith. Harry Beckwith heads Beckwith Partners, a marketing firm that advises twenty-three Fortune 200 clients and dozens of venture-capitalised start-ups on branding and positioning. A Phi Beta Kappa graduate of Stanford, Beckwith is an internationally acclaimed speaker. He is the bestselling authors of five books

BHAG, Big Hairy Audacious Goal is from the book, Built to Last: Successful Habits of Visionary Companies written by Jim Collins and Jerry I. Porras. (New York: HarperBusiness, 1994)

Leveraging The Eco-Wisdom™

Tips for communicating with four behavioural styles is drawn from Assessments 24x7. www.assessments24x7.com

Alignment Check™ is inspired by Gino Wickman's People Analyzer in his book, *TRACTION, Get a Grip on Your Business* (Dallas: BenBella, 2011)

The **HPC** Compass™

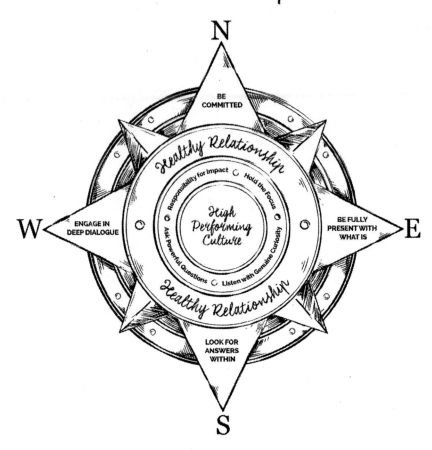